NOTES OF A
PIANO TUNER

NOTES

OF A

PIANO TUNER

Denele Pitts Campbell

PINEAPPLE PRESS, INC.
Sarasota, Florida

The stories contained herein are true. Some names of people and places have been changed.

Inquiries should be addressed to:
Pineapple Press, Inc.
P.O. Box 3899
Sarasota, Florida 34230

LIBRARY OF CONGRESS CATALOGING IN PUBLICATION DATA

Campbell, Denele Pitts, 1948–
        Notes of a piano tuner / Denele Pitts campbell.
                p.   cm.
        ISBN 1-56164-127-8 (alk.paper)
        1. Campbell, Denele Pitts, 1948-   . 2. Piano technicians—
Unites StatesMBiography.   I. Title.
ML429.C165A3 1997
786.2'19'092—dc21
[B]   96-49856
                                                         CIP
                                                         MN

First Edition
10 9 8 7 6 5 4 3 2 1

Design by Carol Tornatore
Printed and bound by The Maple Press Company, York, Pennsylvania

Dedicated to my parents:

Carmyn Gem Morrow Pitts, who gave me the words,

and

Floyd Denver Pitts, who gave me the music,

to my song.

Acknowledgments

I'd like to thank my children, Deste, Jeb and Kadie — and their father Steve — for their patience first as I learned the trade of piano tuning, then as I built the business and rode this wild horse I had roped. They never gave up on me, making kid demands with humor and persistence over the years, even as I moved on to revel in another trade, writing. Also, I'd like to thank my dad for the talent and drive in his lifetime of music and teaching, which he generously gave to me, along with tools, clientele, and reputation, but mostly I thank him for the ethic to take care of the *people*. I'd like to thank the Piano Technicians Guild, whose philosophy demands technical skill and personal integrity, and whose registered technicians — a credential I earned — not only keep America in tune but also take the time to teach and learn from each other. Without the Guild, my professional craft would not have grown. I'd like to thank the countless people whose lives I have crossed, some only once, others many times, who have called me in good faith, welcomed me into their homes, and graciously offered me that drink of water, or to turn off the noisy fan, or to quiet the dog, or the multitude of other concessions that made my work easier. Without the people and their pianos, their dreams of music, my work and this book would never have happened. For keeping me on the road, engine running, I want to thank the special people at University Auto Service. And finally, I'd like to thank my publisher, who picked me up as I wandered the vast, bewildering world of books looking for a friendly face.

Contents

NOTES OF A
PIANO TUNER

Introduction

The Ozark mountains of Arkansas were found-
ed over one billion years ago as a sudden extrusion of
molten red granite and are one of the oldest land forma-
tions in North America. They rise up in a dome of land,
spreading from eastern Oklahoma toward St. Louis in the
northeast, from mid-Missouri in the north down to Little
Rock in the south. Over five hundred million years of sub-
sequent erosion wore down the dome, rain slicing across
the lava, until ocean overtook it and spent the next three
hundred million years laying down sea bed, layer on layer of
sea life and mud and sand and vegetation. Fossilized in the
limestone are the disks of crinoids and fragments of coral,
exposed to view in rough relief against the pale rock that
once was sand and mud, now lying high along the tops and
edges of the mountains.

At the end of the ocean cycles, unexplained geographic
pressures pushed the land up to nearly two thousand feet
above sea level, creating the Ozark plateau. There it sat sub-
jected to the vagaries of the climate, pressured by glacial ice
at the north end and eroded by the melt waters at the south

end, for the succeeding three million years. The limestone was undercut, carved out and eaten away by the runoff from the glaciers, resulting in a labyrinth of caves and underground streams that flow toward the Gulf of Mexico.

Some of the original sea bed plateau collapsed as it was undermined by the glacial rivers, producing narrow valleys where the rivers surfaced after the collapse to flow on top of the land. As the land fell along the waterways, huge sections of the limestone, embedded with its fossils, crumbled into a no-man's-land of steep rocky hillsides strewn with the chunks of rock that are torn between their home strata and the forces of gravity.

Where the glacial rivers raged the strongest, the valleys are wide and the soil has grown deep from silting. Networks of underground caves and waterways crop out along the larger riverbanks, or higher up along bluff walls. Human settlements dating to 7500 BC were among these bluff caves, where bone tools and woven straw baskets have been found. Successive aboriginal occupations are barely documented. Only Osage tribes are known to have roamed the hills in the days just preceding the arrival of Europeans.

White settlers of the late eighteenth and early nineteenth centuries were predominately of Scottish or Irish descent, perhaps drawn to a land so old and so gray and green, like their own homeland, where only the hardiest could force the thin mountain soil to host a few pigs, where their daily work could clear rich bottom land to grow oats or tobacco or corn. Their progeny were fiercely independent, founding simple subsistence farms in choice valleys and on spring-fed mountain tops where they raised large families by the strict rules of Protestant religion.

Today, northwest Arkansas hosts a rapidly growing population of young families, professionals, and retirees who join the heirs of the earliest settlers to produce a thriving economy. Improved highways into northwest Arkansas have opened the area to an influx that was previously restricted by the ridge of mountains along the east and south. The region supports agriculture, forestry, retailers, and manufacturing, as well as the University of Arkansas campus at Fayetteville. There is a dedication among the majority of the region's citizenry to maintain a high quality of life, urging strong environmental protection for the clean waters, pristine natural lands and still-abundant wildlife.

There has always been music in the Ozarks, simple country songs fiddled and sung by first settlers, church hymns that swelled from the keyboards of tiny reed organs, songs of love and of the nation brought forth from gathered choirs. The traditions run strong, infecting natives and newcomers alike. At the gatherings in old community buildings down long miles of dirt road, no foot is still when the fiddle hits the melody and the piano throws the beat of "Arkansas Traveler." In the schools, churches, performance halls, and family rooms (where the music is as much a part of the family as blood kin) the piano continues — as it has for over a century — to preserve the people's musical passion.

Pianos

I never intended to be a piano tuner. While growing up, my life as a female seemed destined to include marriage and children, with a career only to be used in case of emergency as it had been when my mother taught school for a few years to help out in between kids. Being a teacher, then, was the appropriate career, and it was this destiny that led me through college for a Bachelor's degree in secondary education.

Teaching music, however, was my father's profession. He had struggled through a bare-bones country life, enabled by his musical talent to play piano or fiddle for a dance, sing for radio shows, or tune the church piano with makeshift tools. His little jobs helped his parents pay off their home at Cane Hill and kept him fed and in at least one pair of shoes as he worked his way through college in hard Depression times. By 1939, he was teaching music (public school music, piano, band, orchestra, choir) at Rogers High School (northwest Arkansas) for eighty dollars per month.

As his oldest child, my duty was laid before me, first with piano lessons, then clarinet, then oboe, then voice. We sat hours side by side on the piano bench while he made me hear the alto line in one church hymn after another, until in any piece I could discern which notes I should sing for the alto part instead of mindlessly shrilling along with the sopranos. I could barely endure these teaching sessions; his forceful demands on my attention and budding skill exhausted me and left me tense and unhappy.

The music itself transported me. Whenever I could escape dishes, laundry, homework, and other duties that fell on me as the oldest of five, I would struggle with the primitive record player and its thirty-year-old needle to play my father's 78s. There I heard Stravinsky's *Firebird Suite*, Ravel, Brahms, Gershwin. My favorite was Beethoven's *Pathetique*, imagining as the music pounded through the tinny speakers that the story it told was of human loneliness, loss, death. That seemed an appropriate interpretation, in line with the title which I assumed meant "pathetic." Levity seemed spare in the family genes.

I taught school for a year in my chosen field, English, with increasing difficulty. By the end of the year I was positive I would never continue. There were many reasons. I hated being locked in one place all day, every day. I was infuriated by the mandated teaching material, which allowed no creative input from the teachers who might need to tailor a class to suit the needs of the students. I saw years stretching out before me in repetitive frustrations: "be quiet," "sit still," "where is your pencil," "take this note to the office."

I wandered then, taking one job or another, married, divorced, remarried. Secretary, sales clerk, gas station owner. I came in occasionally to assist my now-aging father in his piano tuning work, a full-time job for him in the first years after retirement from teaching. I would organize his desk, return calls, sweep, pick up and put away the myriad tools, bits of felt, leather, brass springs, odds and ends that seemed to collect on every surface of his workshop. He would call on me to come help hold a clamp, come watch him do this or that, until I became familiar with first one aspect and then another of piano repair. He assigned me more and more work, as my time permitted.

And so it was that I learned to be a piano tuner. It was only the financial pressure, my need for income that I could earn in between having babies, that pushed me through those first irritating lessons. It was dirty work, my feet cold even in two pairs of socks as I stood for hours gluing tiny parts together in his little garage shop. I would go home with torn up hands and aching legs. I saw it as a temporary occupation, serving me only until my husband could get a better job.

Now, twenty years later, divorced again and dependent on myself for support, I can't imagine a better career. I've been successful in rising to the top of the field, at least here in northwest Arkansas. The children are mostly grown, but still I luxuriate in a vocation which gives me the freedom to set my own timetables, my own days off. I thrive on the daily variety, driving from home to home, school or church, never too long in one place, always enchanted by the beauty of the Ozarks passing by my windshield, usually intrigued by the people and their lives, challenged by the pianos and their needs. I am, for the most part, satisfied.

Each day teaches me something new, gives me a glimpse into someone else's reality that may be very different from my own. When I enter a home, I am looking for clues that will tell me whether I am preparing the instrument for someone who has spent years practicing the finer nuances of Mozart or if an eight-year-old alone will face the keys to learn the position of middle C. Will I be asked to compromise professional standards just so my work is affordable? Will I be expected to prepare the piano for an artist's touch?

The piano itself is no clear signal of its owner's wealth or expertise. There are plenty of very talented pianists whose hands are frustrated by keys that sit unevenly, ivories cracked and yellowed, the ancient varnish chipped rough and black on a cabinet bruised by frequent moves, its front marked with light green, then white, then brown paint where the movers jostled it through tight doorways. There is no money for a better instrument, and even practice time is stolen in moments between the job frying hamburgers and the rehearsal with the struggling jazz band that may or may not someday earn its keep.

And there are plenty of fine pianos, sitting regally on Persian carpets and polished floors, their nice white and black key tops straight and even and clean, the gleaming lid propped up to reveal glowing copper and steel strings, red and alabaster felts, waiting for someone to come, sit, and play — in a house where no one knows a note. In the right season, for the right occasion, a pianist might be hired to perform for an evening's event, when the people will circulate in their silks and velvets, holding cocktails or fine wine in crystal glasses.

So many times, as I have been standing at the piano striking the keys methodically one at a time, first up to the highest note, then down to the lowest note, jarring the string and wrestling the tuning hammer on each tuning pin into precise musical discipline, I have wondered what story the piano itself would tell of its life. How many times in its early days, before radio, before telephone, were there joyful family gatherings, crowded around the tall piano, singing for Susie's birthday or standing with warm steaming cups of hot cider in hand to shout forth still another refrain of "Deck the Halls"?

I see ghosts at pianos, perhaps a young woman who sat on the maroon velveteen-covered stool, her long taffeta skirts tucked decorously around her delicate legs, her small white hands stretching across the keys to play "Annie Laurie" for her swain attending nearby on the Victorian settee. Or I imagine a busy country mother, drying her hands on her flour sack towel and coming to encourage the practicing child to try again to find the F-sharp, her long hair falling out of its hastily braided knot, her freshly butchered chickens chilling in spring water outside on the cellar steps.

To me, tuning aging pianos in sparse frame buildings scattered around the countryside along narrow dirt roads, there are ghosts who sit in these small church houses, the rural community's cemetery a few yards away. They wait in quiet grief while the minister's wife slowly spreads her plump hands across the keys, playing "The Old Rugged Cross" while a few from the local congregation sing the words in sonorous harmony. The dear one lies dead still in his Sunday suit, hair carefully combed, callused hands folded on his chest, his worries over broken dreams, hard work, unfinished fences, and the fall harvest finally laid to rest, his good and ardent spirit finally free to soar in the ether with the host of the Lord.

The entire pageant of human life, parceled out in half notes and eight-measure phrases, marches across the side meadows of my mind as I find each string's pitch, argue with its stubborn intention to immediately return to its previous sour intonation. When I come here in winter months, the boards of these old churches seem shrunken with the cold and the piano stands stiffly in its place to give warm service on the one day out of seven when the people still come, turn on the fires, shake hands. Their presence lingers and mingles with the ghosts.

There is rich variety in the types of homes I visit. The texture of each occupant's doings speaks to me in detailed clarity: vibrant clusters of flowers growing red, orange, and white in deep green foliage by the front walk of an aging country house; or yellow silk pillows tossed across the white brocade and mahogany fainting couch placed near the spotless white brick fireplace of a lakeside estate; or scattered children's toys, bright colored and jumbled in careless position near the doorway to the kitchen where earnest young voices wonder to their mother what that lady is doing to the piano.

In some homes that stand in rural isolation in the shadow of tall trees, framed against the nearby wintering pastures where fat black cows in the pale short grass observe my arrival in cold torpor, the piano is the heart of the house. Usually it is an old, tall, upright instrument of some vague name like "Netzow" or "Whitney." Its top lid might hold a dusty arrangement of plastic pink roses set in a white and pink swirled glass vase, the special photographs of children and grandchildren, old hymn books and tattered pages of music that was popular during the war. Scattered along the dark varnished surface of the piano's top lie the assorted trivia of a modern world not fully understood — the odd battery, a plastic piece broken off the oven door handle, a key that fits a lock no one can remember. There are hairpins, pencils, letters from friends. There's a borrowed Tupperware dish, left from the last church dinner, and a flashlight to use when the local power supply is knocked out by a storm throwing sheets of icy rain and dead tree limbs down across the yard in its howling possession.

Here in the home of such a piano I know comfort, a kinship borne of my forebears' lives in houses like this. Perhaps the ice is crisp in the tall grass along the driveway fence as I swing my heavy tool case out of my car. I walk along a handbuilt path of wide, smooth native stones toward the house where people were born, married, and died for more than one generation of dirt poor Ozark living, and I greet the ugly dogs sleeping on the porch.

There is a familiarity in the worn, faded carpet lying across the uneven floor. The woman of the house, her skin freckled and soft, her graying hair pushed impatiently back from her cheeks, bustles around me, bringing a tall glass of spring water from her kitchen. She points out the keys where the ivory has come off and then leaves me to work as she finishes the morning dishes. I hear her talking to her old, yellow cat who sits patiently near the doorway between the living room and the kitchen.

In a house like this my grandmother lived, her table scarves embroidered with cardinals and blue morning glories, her clay pots of shamrock, geranium, coleus, and wandering jew crammed into windowsills. Now in this customer's house the window panes are frosted against the frigid wind that rattles the back porch door and hurls the old, black woodstove's plumes of smoke across the gray sky. Here on any Sunday afternoon my grandmother's table would have been set with unmatched, chipped dishes steaming with turnip greens, creamed corn, green beans, tomato gravy, fried chicken, mashed potatoes, hot biscuits, and cherry pie, remnants left after dinner under thin cotton towels in case someone wants to wander back to pick at another crisp, salty thigh, another crusty golden biscuit piled thick with sweet butter and blackberry jam. Someone settles on the creaking piano bench to play quietly, a little slow ragtime, a few songs of the Old South, while others nap, sitting upright on the sagging maroon couch.

At these homes, my tuning time passes swiftly. I am lost in a reverie of poignant thoughts. But even in homes that don't feel familiar, I inadvertently find moving evidence of remarkable lives and intriguing curiosities that occupy my mind and dwell in my memory. I sometimes see my professional duty as an almost sacred task, a ministration to eternal muses which give music to speak what words cannot say in questions or answers that are never clearly formed.

A New Start

*F*or me, working in this field is lavishly ornamented by my fortunate residence in the Arkansas Ozarks. The rich texture of the countryside spreads out in front of me as I travel down the highways and back roads, winding past rushing streams that tumble down steep, rocky hillsides. There are green pastures quietly fitted between the forceful hills where the streams have widened slightly, and meandering stands of white-bark sycamore trees slice through the greenery of the valley grass.

Where the sharp slope of the hills pours down into the flat bottom land, massive gnarled oaks form shaded glades, and the open ground underneath their thick canopy is studded with clusters of young cedars. A few fallen boulders stand among the underbrush, their pale gray serenity sprinkled with green and brown doilies of moss. Up the hillside from these fallen giants and their oak guardians, the exposed rock strata stand high along the ridge, the towering gray cliffs worried by crevices and pressure cracks and cedar roots tenaciously seeking water and sustenance in the dirt-silted openings.

The land excites me. Sometimes I think I value what I see driving from job to job as much as, or more than, the money I receive in payment for my professional services. Scheduling appointments for rural work is like plotting the route for a vacation. Familiar landmarks spring to my mind, perhaps a remarkable vista or dark thicket of woods beckoning me. Each job, like the trip south of town yesterday, is a joyful adventure.

It was a thirty-minute highway drive before I came to the turnoff that would eventually lead me to the home where I would work. There, as the woman had said rather anxiously when she called, I would find a piano badly in need of tuning. Mrs. Landreth said she and her husband had retired from the Detroit area recently, and the piano had been in storage while their new home was being built, which took much longer than they had anticipated. She was concerned, she said, about whether the piano was damaged or if it could be tuned.

I glanced alongside the road as I drove. I had passed a few houses and several driveways that trailed off enigmatically along the faces of hills or dove deeply into thick stands of sumac, young oak, hickory, and locust. This particular road was one I hadn't traveled before, an intriguing turn of events that I always enjoy.

Once the road climbed up the hillside from the valley, there was flat hilltop land, a specialty of the Ozarks. Travelling straight along the fenced pasture edges, the road required some concentration in my driving. Holes opened by rain and speeding tires spread like checkers on a worn checkerboard along the rocky dirt roadway, and some holes spanned the width of the road — muddy pondettes of rainwater with hidden rocks among the sludge along the bottom. Most held a soft spot in the lower side where the water drained off in seepage into the leaf litter and blackberry roots that long since filled the ditch. I watched for the main tracks, following the course set by those who drove back and forth here daily, trusting their choice about which chuckholes to go around or where to ford the pondettes.

Soon, after a few miles along the hilltop pastures and following the steep, curving road down another hillside, the hardwood forest dense on either side, I arrived at the turnoff to my destination, a narrow, rutted lane which veered off to the left from the main county road. I could see the evidence of recent work, culvert pipe newly laid across the ditch and stacks of fresh firewood ricked-up against the trees where there had been clearing for the roadway and the power line right-of-way. It was another addition to our increasing population, another intrusion into deer land and hawk meadows.

The Landreth's drive wound along a narrow creek-bottom valley for a mile or so, sometimes barely squeezing between the hard rock bluffs on my left and the tumbling drop-off some fifty feet down to the water on my right. Further on, the drive dropped into the valley, which opened sufficiently to host a glade of young sycamore, their white scaling bark and pale emerald leaves stark against the deep green woods farther behind as they stood in the yellow sunlight. Bright green grass and tangles of undergrowth thrust up around huge fallen rocks, and as I passed through the pale light it seemed that I had slipped into a magical realm, a world separate from any I had ever known. It pulled on me, as if I could simply leave my car, walk about in it, and take on a new life form of my own.

The long house sat against the side of the narrow valley,

well above the creek. Pulling the car up along the still-loose gravel drive beside the front of the house, I noticed how the brown wooden siding and tan roof blended with the shady bark of the surrounding trees. It will blend even better, I thought, when the newness of the foundation cement doesn't stand out in stark contrast to the dark earth around it, and when a few flower beds and shrubs have grown in against the house to tuck it into the hillside.

There was abundant firewood ricked inside the adjoining carport, testimony to the energy and sudden freedom of the man of the house, I supposed. I noted the car, a fairly new Toyota station wagon. A big Irish setter ambled out from his resting place beside the house to check my arrival.

I gathered up my invoice book and tool case from the back seat of my car, then walked toward the front door while speaking in friendly tones to the aging setter. I've learned over the years to be relaxed and friendly with dogs, which has helped me avoid nasty encounters. They mostly leave me alone after that first amiable exchange. Only once have I been bitten, in a sneak attack to my right Achilles tendon by an over-amped Chihuahua. It was a shock at first to realize the psychotic bony thing had actually bitten me. The vicious little creature's teeth twisted and tugged in my ankle flesh, and I immediately and instinctively prepared to tear him loose and drop-kick him across the yard. Only the sudden appearance of its owner crooning sweet things to it and coaxing it away from me curtailed my reflex action and saved the savage rat-beast.

There was no such threat from the setter, and as we moved up the concrete sidewalk his patient gait a few feet behind me was reassuring. After only a few seconds at the screened porch, I heard footsteps and then Mrs. Landreth opened the house door. She came right out across the porch and opened the outer door for me, talking in greeting, asking if I'd had trouble with the road, or, perfunctorily, if the dog had been any problem. Her demeanor was gentle, intelligent, gracious.

The clean, faintly wood-smoke scented interior welcomed me as I stepped into the house behind her. There was another smell, one that reminded me of a hospital corridor, but it was a passing scent, and I was soon standing in the spacious living room. Comfortable chairs and couches revealed a lifestyle of ease, with photographs of family groups and young children on the natural wood mantle. The small spinet piano stood near the wall, surrounded by shelves artfully arranged with many books, artifacts, a vase or two, several ceramic pots of violets, and a seashell collection. The large, square coffee table, nestled cozily on a thick area carpet, was scattered with various magazines and a couple of pots of rich green, thriving plants.

Mrs. Landreth stood nearby as I played a few octaves. There was nothing startling or even unusual about the response. I knew there was no worry about the piano. I quickly removed the top and front panels and stood them against the bookshelves. I examined the hammers and dampers and the backs of the keys. Everything seemed in order, and I turned to her to reassure her that the piano just needed some tuning, perhaps a little cleaning, and it would be fine.

She relaxed, and a passing expression on her face revealed something to me that seemed more than relief for a piano. I wondered if the instrument involved some special family memory, or if it was a gift from someone. Maybe its original owner had died. I hear these things from people. The piano becomes the receptacle of emotion too heavy to carry around.

I asked to use her vacuum, and if she would bring me a slightly damp dust cloth. She watched me start to work, apologizing that the piano had been so neglected. Not only was it in storage for those eighteen months of the house building, but also had sat here in this room for several months since they had moved in. So many things had happened, she went on, so many things to take care of, the piano had just had to wait.

Time must usually pass quietly here, I thought. She seemed a little anxious for company. I went ahead with my work while I conversed with her so as not to encourage an extended conversation that would interfere with my work schedule. Tuning has to be done in silence, or as close to it as possible, because the tuner must listen to fast or slow vibrations created when sound waves from the piano's notes produce conflicting wave patterns. I've learned how to let people know I need to be left alone, and she, like most, got the message and excused herself.

She soon got busy in the kitchen, working methodically at the cutting board and then at a sizzling pan until the aroma of beef and garlic and onion and celery wound past my nose. Perhaps a pot of stew, I thought. Note by note I made my way up and down the keyboard, wielding my tuning hammer on pin after pin without conscious thought. Somewhere in the years of tuning my capability became ingrained, and I drift off in thought while my inner mind focuses on getting each string in tune.

This is when my eyes roam the walls, shelves, and tables of the room, appreciating the collection of Dickens, the volumes on history, the copies of *National Geographic*. On her mantle, I looked into the eyes of many faces frozen in time, framed in wood, brass, and silver, sitting in careful arrangement along the long shelf. Grandparents, or even great-grandparents, standing soberly in their finest clothing, the man seated and the woman standing, her small hand carefully laid across his shoulder where the thick, black woolen jacket pulled smoothly from the stiff collar to the fitted sleeve. His beard was dark and carefully trimmed close to his strong jaw, and her light hair was pulled back too severely from her thin face. In another, the family group stood by a buckboard wagon, the rough boots on the men and the women's raw cotton dresses defining the character even if the flinty stares and seamed faces would not.

The piano's mahogany cabinet was well polished, almost certainly brought into this family brand-new in the late 1950s when the first of their three or four children reached eight years of age and could start piano lessons. Left behind as the children have probably grown and married and moved to Indiana or Colorado, the piano stood as a part of the remaining family life, an investment of hope and love and not insignificant finances. Memories of piano teachers and recitals and emotional practice schedules were as firmly attached to its frame as the layers of furniture polish, a repository of life energy written in halting Mozart.

Some of the keys in the high end were sluggish, a sure sign to me that no one had been playing those notes. I interrupted the kitchen activities of Mrs. Landreth and asked whether it was played much, and she confirmed my guess that she only played on occasion, that perhaps the grandchildren would play when they visit on holiday. There was a pause, and again I got the idea that there was something not said. She'd like to play more, she said then, and that's why she's decided to have it tuned. I showed her how the high notes didn't return rapidly enough and explained that more use would help lubricate those tiny brass pins the moving parts swing on, and I encouraged her to play it more. She hesitated, obviously struggling with some inner conflict, before telling me that her husband had a serious stroke about two months earlier, and that she had him here to take care of now. Therefore, she finished a little sadly, she didn't have as much time to do things she had planned, like playing the piano, maybe learning to play as well as he had.

I nodded, only briefly but sincerely expressing my condolences for her and her husband's difficult state of affairs, and then gave her some emotional space, freedom to go back to the kitchen, freedom for me to tune the piano. After all, I was only a piano tuner, and how much of her feelings and the suffering of her husband would she really want to share with a stranger. My mind went back over the things I had seen there: the wood cut and ricked, the care taken with the grounds to clear brush and dead limbs, the oversight of driveway building and house construction, all of it cut fresh into this hidden little valley. I wondered about this man who waited decades, worked hard at his job, made an enduring marriage and raised a family, and finally managed to capture the prize, time to play his piano among the tall oaks and gray cliffs and rushing stream, only to be slapped down with a debilitating stroke.

I wondered if she would manage alone like this for long, depending on herself and a part-time day worker for shopping, cooking, care taking, and remaining sane. Soon, my work was finished and the corner of their living room now a familiar outpost in my mind's eye as I reassembled the piano and closed up my tool case. I took a last look out the large sliding glass door which opened onto a deck, a view they would see every day while playing the piano or if they sat on their living room couch to read their books or stare at the fire in their fireplace.

The wide glass panes faced out over the trunks of the tall oaks and a few locusts which reached up toward the day that was spilling over the top of the mountains. The pale growth of seeded grass on the grounds of the small, tended yard seemed tenuous at best, the precise flower beds freshly planted in red geranium and violet petunias oddly incongruous on the uneven ground that sloped from the sharp hillside down across the yard to the rocky creek bank. Beyond it the jumble of rocks along the rushing stream confirmed the natural order of the land. I moved toward the front hallway.

I spoke Mrs. Landreth's name, and she came out a partially closed doorway a little way down the hall. I could see behind her through the opening, the white sheets and the half-propped-up hospital bed. I saw the movable little table/tray, its chrome frame shining softly in the light of the room. I saw the man, his face slack and pale as he lay back against the pillows. His eyes didn't look up toward me, and I ended my quick glimpse in hopes that neither she nor he would feel any intrusion from my curiosity.

She came briskly toward me, and I handed her the bill. She excused herself, and when she returned with her checkbook, she talked briefly while she made out the check, about how long it took to feed him, but how much better it was now that he could be fed through his mouth. I didn't ask anything further, but I tried to let her know how I hoped things would improve.

He has a chance, she said, for a full recovery, but not a

good one. She handed me the check, and I slipped it into my invoice folder. He might never be able to walk or talk, she said. She guessed she would sell this and move into town if it turned out that way. I picked up my tools and moved toward the door. I told her it was good that they had gained a few months of life here before this happened, and she agreed. I didn't know what else to say. I told her to call in about a year for another tuning.

Driving slowly back, I wondered if she screamed at the trees at night, if she blamed the house and land and retirement for his stroke, if she wept at the window at ten in the morning. The land and trees and weathered rocks seemed quieter now than they had on my way toward the house, as if my new knowledge of human pain had laid a thin veil over it all. The high bluffs loomed along the valley edge as I eased down the narrow lane, and after some time, when I once again turned onto the highway for the last quick leg back to town, I diverted my wondering to what I would fix for dinner.

3

Parenting with Piano

In some homes I work alone, the husband and wife both off for the day in their own cars to wrest another fifty or a hundred dollars from the tight fist of the city, children in the nearby school, the family dog barking from his frustrated post in the garage at my rude invasion of his territory. I see the notes left for when school is out, when the children amble home to the empty house to stand in front of the open refrigerator, pondering the day-old Jell-O, the tired bologna, the last bit of French onion dip before going to the television to watch a mindless blur of cartoons, car chases, Pepsi ads.

In this house I am an expensive luxury, called because the piano is a remnant of a more genteel day when the stay-home mother had hot chocolate ready for kids returning from school, when music studies defined a proper middle-class life. Now the piano is barely afforded, reclaimed from an aunt's parlor and replete with mouse dumplings under the keys, moth holes puncturing the felts, and the faded gold lettering on the fallboard declaring its origins: "Hobart M. Cable, Upright Grand, Chicago."

The keys are hard to play, and at best the tuning will hold for six months. I cannot give them what they need, a smoothly operating machine that will spill forth sweet tones to the sparing efforts of little hands in a last-ditch effort to build personal skill and discipline in a world where a flip of a button brings forth perfect, pre-recorded music, where every shopping trip, every movie, every car ride is saturated with symphonies, voices, and scales too great, too vast to ever be accomplished by this little child or this crumbling instrument.

I give a little extra on these jobs, trying my best to support their good intentions. I find myself accommodating the people more than the instrument, cutting corners to just get all the keys to work, or tuning below pitch so it will cost the minimum. When the opportunity arises, I communicate my support for their effort at music training for their children, perhaps mentioning how hard it is for kids to practice since the piano lessons compete with the other things they like. I mention all the advantages of lessons, like learning perseverance and self-discipline, in hopes that the harassment the parents experience paying for lessons, driving back and forth to lessons, and overseeing daily practice doesn't overcome the desire for their child to play piano.

Statistically, though, I know piano is losing. Kids taking lessons have decreased in number steadily for thirty years. Similarly, new piano sales have dropped. Television, tapes and compact disc, radio, and Sega games have taken over. I wonder if I should encourage my children to learn my trade. Maybe there won't be enough piano tunings in thirty more years to keep a business going.

Every so often I find myself up against a piano that is too far gone, and I cannot be accommodating. It's an impossible situation. That's when it sat in the carport and took blowing rain for six years, when the veneer is buckled and bulging out from the sides, when the keys are swollen and stuck against each other and the ivories long since have fallen off. The piano is a basket case, but it's all they've got and they want it to work. When it truly is beyond hope, I have to say no, there's nothing I can do.

Or in other piano deaths, the instrument may have sat for years in Granny's barn, its steel casters buried in the dirt floor and termites eating their way up the soundboard. A giant rat nest is couched inside the upper cabinet, composed of chewed-up hammer felts, key wood, and bits of leather from the parts in the mechanism. Many strings have broken from the rust collected in deep red granules near the tuning pins, and the whole pinblock has pulled forward, separated from the wooden support posts in the back, under the pressure of long-taut strings.

There is no hope for these, and I advise the customer to just take it to the landfill. Maybe some of the cabinetry can be salvaged; maybe we'll try to save some of the veneer to patch damaged spots on pianos we restore in the shop. It's never a nice situation, like seeing an old lion, toothless and weak with age, who can only suffer until a merciful caretaker puts him down.

On occasion, a piano will have just enough life left to merit consideration. Not that it would be worthy for an accomplished pianist who expected to execute Chopin or Rachmaninoff, but it might bear up a few more years to serve as a crippled soldier in the war among parents with no money, their dreams of a better world, and kids who want to learn to play. In my role as diplomat in this conflict, I try to make it clear to the parents that there will be keys that don't work as easily as their neighbors, or notes that won't hold a tune, my point being that in a time when kids may already be predisposed to give up easily, such a failing instrument will only add to the likelihood that the music lessons won't take hold.

None of that matters to the parents. They have no choice. A new piano may cost thousands, another debt to pay off with monthly installments, added to the many others that stack up at the first of every month to consume the paycheck and leave nothing for the dentist, new shoes, or a trip to Disneyworld.

I drove to one home on the north side of town, down a little lane of a housing addition that had passed its prime by 1970. The yard was clean, but rutted by walking paths alongside the crumbling driveway. A woman dressed in a nurse's uniform came to the door and welcomed me in.

Inside the house, standing on threadbare carpet, I saw the clear signs of their poverty: minimal furniture, well worn, only a few books on the shelves, an economy- model television on a chrome stand, veneer peeling on the corners of the coffee table. The piano stood resolutely in the dining room, squeezing the dinette set over against the other wall where a battered reproduction of a landscape painting hung in a scratched frame.

The woman explained that with just her salary to support herself and the three children she can't afford much. Just to drag home this old beast had cost them three hundred dollars. She was hopeful she could get some use out of it since two of her children want to learn to play. I echoed her hope as I stood at the keyboard.

Several keys were sticking, an indication that the house where it sat before may have had too much moisture. Opening the cabinet, I discovered many loose parts, and when I hit a key, the hammer wobbled violently as it traveled toward the string. Releasing the key let the hammer fall back on its tortured path, and the hardened damper felt recontacted the string with a *zzzzzing*. Quickly running a scale up and down the keyboard, I listened for wildly out-of-tune notes, and watched the other eighty-seven hammers travel toward the string and back. Several were broken off, and no note sounded for those keys. Everything was loose, but, amazingly, most notes were close to correct pitch.

Crouching down to remove the kickboard, I noted the middle pedal was missing, not that it mattered much. Most middle pedals serve duplicate function with the right pedal, which lifts the dampers from all the strings and lets the notes ring in sustained sound. With the kickboard out of the way, I began to check inside, looking for cracks in the soundboard or loose seams in the bridges. I was relieved to find there were no serious problems down there, and I began to formulate what it would cost this family for my services, which would involve getting the keys functional and a tuning.

Usually such get-by jobs leave me feeling like I've cheated the customer, taking money for work on a piano that will never perform well. I try to gauge what the instrument's use will be, what the other options are for the people involved, what those other options would cost in comparison to the cost of patch-up work that will result in poor musical performance on a dying piano. I explained to her that the wobbling and *zzzings* would not be remedied cheaply, but if she could endure that, I would at least get all the notes to play. In that case, I estimated minimum repairs and tuning would total one hundred fifty dollars.

She was pleased it could be tuned. I suppose that her fall-back option would have been to use it as it was. She had waited for me to assess the situation before rushing off to her job. She left me a check for the quoted amount and instructions about locking up. The house became quiet, and I started my work. It took about an hour to get all the keys working and another forty-five minutes to tune. I sat down to play a few bits and pieces on the freshly cleaned keys, satisfied that this job was as good as it could be, all things considered. I didn't expect to be called back, since I recognized that in this case the piano budget had been fully expended. They would get by from here on.

On another occasion, I arrived for my appointment on a dark, cold day at a long, bungalow-style house that sat out in the middle of cleared pasture land at the end of a muddy lane. Smoke poured from a metal stove pipe that came up slightly crooked from the back side of the ramshackle house. Several old cars and pickups were clustered around an outbuilding, and three big tan-and-white hound dogs rose up from where they had been huddled on the porch of the house and howled up a greeting. The porch also held the family's freezer, speckled with rust spots, a half rick of firewood, two dilapidated upholstered armchairs, and several odds and ends, boots, fishing poles, a lawn mower.

At the door, an overweight woman with stringy hair met me, her manner polite as she asked me to come in. With a thin brown sweater buttoned up over her cotton blouse, she held her hands together in front of her in a posture reminiscent of supplication, walking with me through the sparsely furnished living room then into the family room where the piano in question stood. She explained how she'd found it at a garage sale for only fifty dollars. Her husband and some of his friends got it home, and now it needed tuning.

The house smelled bad, like a cat litter box mixed with dirty laundry and burned bacon. The stained olive green carpet had bits and pieces of debris scattered across it, and a tattered couch sat over to the left side of the room, facing a television on a little metal stand. A wood-burning stove sat on a loose platform of brick across the room from the piano, in between the couch and the television, and the bricks and floor around it were thick with pieces of bark, slivers of split wood and shavings, a small stack of newspapers, a few sticks of wood. Out the window beside the stove I could see pasture land stretching off to the hills, a scattering of brown cows standing with their rear ends toward the cold wind, the grass killed back to tan with a few intermingled sprinklings of green winter-hardy growth. There was a rust-colored swing set in the backyard nearer the house, and red, yellow, and blue plastic toys scattered across the yard.

A baby began to cry fretfully in the other end of the house, and the woman excused herself while I started looking inside the piano. There were several keys that didn't work, mostly from broken pieces that kept the hammers from hitting the strings. Mice had been at work, and the evidence of their urine sat crystalline on the return spring wires, on the key bushings, on the strings themselves. The whole piano smelled like mice and decay, a moldy rank smell that had soaked into the wood and felts. The keys sat unevenly, like the smile of a seven-year-old child with some teeth missing, some partly grown back in. Most of the notes played, but several required a hard stroke to activate, and others hit weakly, only barely exciting the string. The tuning was a full step below standard pitch, not necessarily a problem with the piano being played by itself, but the lower pitch gave the strings too much slack which caused the bass notes to growl and thump.

I stood there, listening to the dogs barking outside as the woman stayed with the baby. There were footsteps on the porch, and then three children burst through the doorway, arriving home from school. Peeling off their coats and throwing them across the nearby furniture, they swarmed around the piano, two girls and a boy, their eyes shining with questions and curiosity about the insides of the wooden box that had been in their home a month. They held back at first, but I smiled at them, and they asked first one thing and then another. What is this? What is that? I showed them how it worked inside, what the strings were, how they were hit by the hammers, how the keys moved.

The front door slammed again, and their faces reflected a flash of anxiety, awareness of a presence that might demand too much, might lash out suddenly. I heard his brash voice yelling at the kids about their books thrown down on the floor, knew what to expect before his swollen belly came into view. His red plaid flannel shirt was stretched tight across his big beer gut, the buttons pulling against the buttonholes to reveal the dirty T-shirt underneath. There was grease across the thighs of his filthy jeans which sat low under his belly. His fat face challenged me, no smile from his small brown eyes as he asked just what I thought was the least I needed to do.

I'd seen the type before, and I presented my comments with no emotion, but in a tone of authority as if to say that he could either hire my work or not, I wouldn't care. I pointed out the problems, explained briefly the choices he could make, whether to spend one hundred dollars or three hundred dollars or nothing. He said the damn kids had some idea about music lessons; he didn't think they'd amount to anything with it, but the wife had gone out and paid money for this damn thing. Nearly broke his back getting the damn thing into the house. What I could do for fifty dollars would be all it would get, more money than he could afford to pay, and they probably wouldn't stick with it anyway.

No, I added silently, they won't. Not with a piano like this that barely works, that won't hold a tune, especially in a room with a wood-burning stove. Not with an attitude like this going in.

He was proud of his cynicism, glad to know in advance that each and every one of his children would fail to learn music. I narrowed down what I planned to do to the instrument. He felt secure in his view of the world, and he would not change his mind. He soon wandered off through the adjoining kitchen, where he opened the refrigerator and pulled out a can of beer. Slamming out the back door, he went back to his garage and the grease and the privacy, leaving me with my work and the children. Fifty dollars would get the keys in the middle to work and clean up the middle octaves so that their beginning music sounded right. I did that, a short time of work with the quietly attentive children monitoring my every move.

They brought me a glass of cold water, set it carefully on

a nearby table. They quietly watched me take out tools and put them back down, watched me squeeze glue and fit parts back together, listened as the strings were pulled up and down to match tune with their neighbors. They knew what they wanted, the musical muse tempting them with creation. I was breathing life into their sleeping beast, and magic would soon follow.

The woman returned, and she, too, wanted to know what I could do for a reasonable price. I told her the options I had seen, that I had outlined them to her husband, told her what her husband had said. She seemed subdued, resigned, relieved that he would do anything to improve it, said that whatever he said was what I should do.

As the repairs were completed, and the best possible use of the fifty dollars had been spread thin as a film of dust across the instrument, I pulled up a nearby chair to play a few things on the dirty keys. The children were wholly absorbed, a kind of reverent pall cast in the room as "Eleanor Rigby" was forced from the crippled animal, its voice cracked, its feet lame and staggering. But it made the music, its strings forcing their vibrations through the shattered soundboard and loose bridges to carry the song out into the room to the children's eager ears.

I reassembled the banged-up cabinet, ignoring the many things I had left undone. I explained to the woman the best method for cleaning the keys, for making the cabinet look better with a little Old English furniture polish. It was fifty dollar's worth and more, and yet I felt bad taking the money the woman so carefully counted out for me, most likely an expenditure of food money in a life where even the basics were hard earned. I suspected what the man would say, returning later to have his dinner, more beer, the TV, when the children would wait for the right moment, select the bravest of themselves to go the keyboard to play in hopes of his approval, when the first few tentative notes would be struck: "Damn kids."

I knew by the address the woman gave me that the house was in an exclusive neighborhood on the west side of town. The road through that area ultimately reached a dead end after curving up and around the sides of the mountain. The most expansive homes, of course, were built on the mountain's flat Ozark top, where the cleared land yielded a panoramic view of the other hills and valleys to the east and south.

My appointment time was set for 3:30 P.M., since no one would be home before that time to let me in. At this hour, at least the baby-sitter would arrive after picking up the kids from school, and I would be able to tune the piano, which, the woman said on the phone, hadn't been serviced in over a year and certainly needed attention.

I was running a little early that day so I drove slowly along the winding roadway, observing fabulous homes and well-tended grounds that each vied for the award of "best." One split-level sat against the sharply sloped hillside in shades of gray-stained cedar, with a white gravel drive that skirted the tiled pool and the wooded rock gardens. A two-story Tudor in pale pink stood on a flat lot near the top of the hill with its careful gardens laid out in geometric precision, just the right shades of pink and red flowers framed with the trimmed shrubbery.

I arrived at the designated address, still a few minutes

early. I rang the doorbell but the house was empty, so I returned to my car to sit and wait. The concrete drive was meticulously edged with a gravel border, which was in turn edged by a wide, curving bed of ivy. To the east end of the house stood a remnant of the original woods that had possessed the mountain before the real-estate developers came along, now a see-through buffer between this and the next house. There were a few large oaks still standing, left here and there in the yard and behind the house where the architects felt they would serve the aesthetic ideal of the setting.

I studied the house, a sweeping work of timber and rock with a roof line that dipped and flew like some prehistoric bird. I suspected that the interior would house a few fine pieces of art, at least one leather-upholstered chair, perhaps a marbled foyer floor. Glancing up, I caught a sudden glimpse of a small, red car arriving behind me in the drive, and it slipped past me to park in a space closer to the garage.

The petite, college-age blonde came toward me and inquired whether I was the piano tuner, as her wards, two boys and a girl, piled out and gathered their books and jackets. I gave them a few minutes to get into the house before following with my tool case up the sidewalk. The children were well groomed and well dressed in the latest fashion, of course, in jeans that probably cost fifty dollars per pair and sneakers that cost at least seventy-five.

The entry hall floor was not marble, as I had guessed, but a rough-cut dark gray slate. The baby-sitter led me through the long, high-ceilinged hallway which passed the kitchen and dining room before opening into a large recreation room. The floor became covered in a dense oatmeal-colored carpet, complementing the ivory stucco walls. In the middle of the room was a pool table with a domed light hanging down low over its center. A rack of cues was mounted on the nearest wall, and close by was a small bar, complete with stainless steel sink, a few shelves of glasses, and an assortment of liquor bottles.

At the far end of the room stood a fairly new piano, a medium-grade brand that promised me little problem in tuning. I set my tools down beside the music cabinet where I could see mostly beginner's music along with a few books that must have been the property of the parents, such as *Pieces You Love to Play* and the *Reader's Digest Collection of Golden Favorites*. I moved the brass piano lamp off the top lid and set the plaster busts of Bach, Beethoven, and Brahms onto a nearby side table. I scooted the giant potted ficus tree sideways so that it no longer hovered so closely over the end of the piano, and then opened the piano to begin work.

The baby-sitter returned to the kitchen, where the children were clustered, demanding their favorite snacks. I listened to the two boys, probably aged ten and twelve, as they argued about the presidential candidates. Their argument undoubtedly parroted what they had heard from adults, their language peppered with words like "responsible" and "conservative" and "liberal." In between their statements, they requested more Coke, another piece of sausage pizza, another bowl of corn flakes.

The baby-sitter demurred quietly, probably partial to the little girl who quietly murmured about her day at school while the boys carried on their pseudo-discussion. I wondered how late their professional parents came home, whether a housekeeper prepared meals, whether they would travel to the Colorado mountains for vacation, or if perhaps this year they would take a cruise in the Caribbean. I wondered if they had to pick up their own clothes, or if someone came in periodically to clean, launder, and vacuum.

The piano was hardly out of tune, but I gave it a complete going-over to be sure not one note warbled. The hammers were in like-new condition, and I could still smell factory chemicals emanating from the interior as I worked. Within a fairly short time, my work was complete and I put things back in order, including the ficus. I gave a quick dusting to the keys, wrote up the invoice, and left it on top of the piano as I had agreed with the woman of the house over the phone.

The boys had drifted outside, but the baby-sitter was still sitting at the kitchen bar with the little girl as I walked through. I asked who was the piano player, and the little girl in her spotless dress and curling brown hair said that she was, that she had been taking lessons. I asked if she liked it, and she said yes, very much. The baby-sitter beamed at the girl and then asked me if she could do anything for me. No, I said, I was finished. The bill was on the piano, and I would let myself out.

It was an ordered world that I walked through, leaving the house. There were no cobwebs, no dust underneath the expensive side tables that hosted a bronze bust and a Chinese vase. The high windows at the top of the smooth walls let in a quiet light, and the brass doorknob clicked efficiently as I turned it to go out. Were there times when this door was slammed in anger or when the boys felt rowdy and ran outside to play? Was this mother frustrated that she wasn't home with cookies to meet her children after school? Was the father not there except to have political discussions with friends, overheard by his sons and repeated in after-school conversation while other boys talked about their last father-son fishing trip? I would not have answers. It was three weeks before I received their check.

Teachers

*T*eaching music is one of those human endeavors which qualifies one for a special category of sainthood. Suffering daily invasion at their homes, piano teachers must put up a fresh, cheerful face at half-hour intervals, ready for tortured eight-measure phrases that play out note by stammering note. Only a person destined for holy recognition could endure such tedious hope that someday, somehow, this child's hands might play smooth passages of Bach.

Women seem to dominate the field of piano teaching, a relic, no doubt, of old, established cultural norms that left them few options in methods of earning money. Piano instruction suits the traditional female role of homemaker and mother. While her dinner simmers on the stove, while her children dutifully study their homework, she is free to isolate herself in the living room with the piano and the student, and the money earned there provides no threat to the prestigious career of her husband, who arrives home safely after the lessons are completed.

It took me awhile to catch on to the insider information about piano teachers and tuners. And I might have languished in ignorance longer had it not been for Mrs. Spring. I actually was a little intimidated at her first call, since I was still new at the business and rather insecure about my skills.

She was professional in her approach, speaking over the phone in a friendly voice, brisk and to the point. She lived in a small town about an hour's drive from Fayetteville, she said and, after explaining how she had obtained my name and number, inquired whether I would consider driving up to her location. At it happened, I had already committed to some work in that community for the upcoming week, and I was pleased to be able to tell her that yes, I would be glad to service her piano. I set the appointment fairly early in the day, hoping to complete her job and be ready for the other work that I had already scheduled.

On the morning of my appointment with Mrs. Spring, I set out on the narrow, curving road that stretches northward through the hills to that town. I subdued my hurry as the road dawdled through several small communities, each of which importantly posts thirty-five mile-per-hour speed limit signs along the three-quarter-mile stretch between the signs marking the city limits. Worse for me that particular morning was the fact that frequently while driving along the road I had to suddenly slam on the brakes to avoid crashing into a vehicle moving at a remarkably slower speed.

There are old tales about farmers and driving. For example, there's the common notion that farmers drive faster on dirt roads than they do on pavement. A favorite story is the one about the farmer who pulled out onto a busy highway with no regard for the heavy traffic bearing down on him, causing several drivers to swerve, go off the road, and generally break out in cold sweats. One driver, incensed at his near-death experience, followed the farmer to his destination at the local feed store, (so the story goes) where he confronted the old man as he climbed down out of his aging pickup.

"What's the big idea, pulling out on the road like that?" the man demanded angrily.

The farmer squinted toward the man, as if to determine whether this was, in fact, a serious question. "Sonny boy," he finally drawled, "you must be new around here. Why, I turn there every day."

I have conducted my own careful observations of farmer driving habits. My conclusion is that it only *seems* that they drive faster on dirt than they do on pavement. The actual fact is that they drive forty miles per hour no matter where they are. This seems inordinately fast on dirt roads because it results in a big cloud of dust trailing like a jet stream and a certain degree of excitement on sharp corners.

The highway is another matter. Forty miles per hour is absurdly slow, especially when a person like me is already late for an appointment and needs to go at least sixty in order to show up even fifteen minutes late. And such was the case for my first appointment with Mrs. Spring. I had made a late start and was trying to make up for it by zooming down the road as fast as I dared. Inevitably, it is in such situations that the dreaded farmer looms in the road just ahead.

For several reasons, going around this slow-moving obstacle is not possible. The road curves and winds with a double yellow line stretching as far as the eye can see. In the few places where the yellow line relents and a straight stretch opens up, there is invariably an oncoming car. Or the farmer chooses just this moment to stretch the limits of his truck to race along at fifty or fifty-five, perhaps making a kind effort to allow me (and the others who have congregated in an impatient parade behind him) to go a little faster. But in fact his burst of speed simply prevents anyone from managing to go around him.

No amount of foaming at the mouth, questioning his intelligence or parentage, riding up within three feet of his rear bumper, or swerving precipitously in false starts around him seems to deter him from his steady turtle's pace. Perhaps he has some perverse intention in exerting this bit of influence over a world out of control, of slowing things down so that we can all appreciate the purple haze cast among the feathery fall seed heads of the ditch grasses or swerve quickly enough to avoid the various creatures that exercise such poor judgment about when to cross these rural roads.

I had checked my watch for the twentieth time. Already ten minutes late and at least another twenty minutes of road time ahead. There was no place where I might stop to call Mrs. Spring to let her know I was delayed. The miles dripped by while I invented rhetorical questions and devastating insults for the farmer. I inventoried the bits of things that had collected in my car: fast food containers, newspapers, bank deposit envelopes, umbrella, ice scraper, gloves, cassette tapes, a box of tissues, assorted odd pieces of paper. I planned what to fix for dinner. I organized my "to do" list into fifteen-minute increments.

Ultimately, the farmer and the rest of us arrived at the outskirts of town, where he ceremoniously pulled off at the hardware store. Shoving my foot down on the accelerator in a fit of frustrated anger, I swerved around him and raced through town toward Mrs. Spring's.

Speeding down the long curving road toward her house, I barely glanced at the sunlight-dappled road as I busily organized my invoice book, her message slip, and my tool case. Midway through a narrow turn, I saw on the pavement in front of me a tiny bluebird, its blueness rich as royal silk as it lay shattered against the gray pavement. My mind surged with a million responses as I neared the feathered body and only at the very last second did I see the fluttering, frantic ministrations of its mate, hovering only a foot or two above the dead bird, trying probably in some primal intelligence to help the companion that it knew.

I had no options at that eleventh hour, no way to swerve as I faced an oncoming car, no path of escape as I felt with my whole body the force of my car's steel demolish the life in the fluttering bluebird, the partner of the dead one. The life that had remained was stopped cold by me. I wanted to cry out as I felt the impact, magnified as it was by my rage and pain from being so irrevocably swept along by the forces of my time, by my car, by the road, by the lateness of the hour and the expectations of Mrs. Spring, by my need for the money I would get for the job.

I wanted to go home. Instead, I turned into Mrs. Spring's drive. Thirty-five minutes late and in no mood to work, I gathered my tool case and rushed to her door. She greeted me with a serene smile as I hurriedly ranted about getting behind slow traffic. She said it was quite all right, that she would have been there anyway, and not to worry. I was too ashamed to admit the bird incident. She ushered me through her elegant little dining room and the spotless kitchen, down a long flight of stairs, and around the corner to her piano room. As she gently moved around me, taking the music and other items off the piano, I tried to relax. She offered to bring me a drink, then returned upstairs, leaving me with the piano.

The work was not difficult. It was clear that she had taken great care over the years to keep her piano in good condition. Her phone rang at one point while I tuned, and I could hear her voice filtering faintly from the upstairs rooms. I was thankful for her generous nature, her immediate forgiveness for my late arrival, her tidy approach to daily life. Around her piano were the trademark items of her business: the shelves of piano music, the metronome, the sharpened pencils, the calendar of student names and times. I noticed the collection of piano things: a giant eraser in the shape of a note, a group of tiny pianos of glass, wood or ceramic, wall hangings with statements about life and pianos. On a side table sat a tiny glass bluebird, and I moved it behind the lamp so I would not look at it.

I found myself oddly reassured as I sat there tuning Mrs. Spring's piano. Her tranquil presence seemed to emanate from the room and its furnishings, immutably and eternally composed. Through the nearby window, the leaves on the low oak tree branches played slowly in shadow and light.

In the years since that first visit to Mrs. Spring's piano, I have tuned for many other teachers. They seem to collectively hold access to a reservoir of strength and patience which they tap each day in their encounters with their students. I've wondered whether a certain type of person, already imbued with this strength, is preordained for certain fields of work, such as teaching music, or whether the work itself, chosen for any other number of reasons, bestows on its practitioners this inordinate patience. They speak calmly, lovingly. Their eyes sparkle with the certain knowledge that while the majority of their young students might squirm, forget the position of middle C, and regularly fail to practice, a few will connect with the magic of music and flower in its glow. Perhaps more importantly, even those who barely begin to learn music still gain a valued life lesson.

Piano teachers seem to love their work. When all else fails in their lives, the piano teaching continues. Children grow and move away. Husbands die. Times change. The piano teacher remains, as steadfast as the moderato beat of a sonatina.

Of course there are sometimes those who teach for less than ideal reasons. The economy of ten students at thirty dollars apiece per month does not escape the attention of some who aren't so patient or good. One teacher I tuned for had a miserable little spinet with filthy keys and (just judging by the smell) a cat with overactive kidneys. I couldn't understand how anyone would be able to consistently return their children to her house for lessons. One teacher I met carefully escorted me through her expensive living room as though I might pilfer the artwork, seemed unconcerned when I pointed out several problems with the piano, not the least of which was the terrible state of the tuning, and then sniffed at my recommendation that regular tunings were in order.

Several years after my first call on Mrs. Spring I went to tune for a woman who had been the best-known piano teacher in that city for decades. I had heard of her before she ever called me to tell me that her tuner had died and she would like to give me a try. Knowing her reputation, I was a little surprised that the house looked run down, and I knocked twice before it occurred to me that somehow I might be at the wrong address. But the street and number were what she had told me on the phone, and I hesitated a bit longer at the door.

She came to the door then, looking frail, standing in the opening to unlock the clasp on the storm door before backing up slightly to let me step in. The wooden door was only opened enough to allow a person to slip through, and as soon as I stepped into the room, I could see why. Behind the door were stacks of music. And beyond the stacks of music were her two Steinway grands, sitting side by side. Not that one could readily determine what they were.

Not only was music stacked behind the front door, it was heaped across the tops of both pianos, and the stacks flowed together into a sea of music that continued onto nearby shelves and the floor on the other side, obstructing the passageway into the rest of her house. There was a narrow trail that led from the door alongside the piano benches and toward the hallway and a second path that veered toward the center of the room to the couch, where just enough space had been left for her to sit. It took twenty minutes and probably the entire reserve of her day's energy to unload enough space on the front of the pianos so that I could simply tune. There were assignment cards, notes from parents, paper clips, and shiny little sticky stars in red, blue, silver, and gold jumbled among the endless pages of music. Clearly, life had overwhelmed her.

She hovered from her slot on the couch behind me while I tuned and carefully checked my tuning with slow scales on both instruments before giving me a crisp nod and asking for my bill. All surfaces in the room were covered, I realized as I looked around, with not only music, but shopping bags, mail, newspapers, magazines, and an endless list of other things. The stacks on the floor between her slot on the couch and the television screen were graduated in height so that when leaning back, she could just see the screen. Shocked as I was at the crushing volume of her belongings, I still found her approach fascinatingly efficient.

I suffered some concern that she didn't find my work satisfactory when I did not get another call from her, but a couple of years later I found out she had only lived a few months past my visit. She had been ninety-three at the time.

Some are so generous with their talents that they are willing to teach for public schools. School pianos are without doubt some of the worst I have ever serviced. The instruments are often fairly new, but injured with carved initials, spilled soda pop, too-hot or too-wet environments, and repeated movings by energetic fifteen-year-old boys who have no concern about crashing the piano across high thresholds and into door frames. Out of these mauled, rarely-tuned instruments, public school music teachers must coax inspiration and melody with one hand, while with the other hand direct the restless assemblage of kids through the indecipherable codes of the music printed on the pages of their music books.

School administration seems never to appreciate the importance of music, unless it is to provide rousing marches and pep songs at appropriate intervals of athletic events. Music teachers, dedicated students, and a few parents end up working exhausting hours at concession stands or selling

Christmas cards and T-shirts just to get enough money for band uniforms and one or two more music selections to play. Music is taken for granted, a fine background for the more important workings of modern life, but rarely the featured budget item on the school board list.

Several piano teachers I have known worked first for the schools. They held a vision of what music could do for the children: give them organization in the workings of their growing minds, inspire them, offer them a lifetime of pleasure and appreciation. After a certain time, these teachers' energy was gone, sucked out by diminishing funds, lack of equipment, and the repeated insults of being relegated to a part-time status or having their school day schedules split between two schools. The ideal of teaching was supplanted by the need for personal survival.

It is the children who suffer. In the fastest-growing city of this region the school district has been struggling to keep up with enrollment. Almost every year they open a new elementary school, only to discover on the second or third day of class that it is already over full. When I began servicing their pianos at the early stages of this growth, each elementary school had its own music room, with a nice piano and shelves where careful arrangements of music books, instruments, and charts provided a generous learning environment. Now, the music teachers are reduced to pushing a record player on a cart from room to room, playing recordings for fifteen-minute sessions of "music appreciation." The piano is shoved against the wall of the cafeteria, used only on the rare occasion when the children might be encouraged to sing.

Eventually, many music teachers retreat from the onslaught of such mediocrity. In their homes, they can create an atmosphere that treasures music, that values the effort of each child who enters. The pace is their own and gives enough time so that a bond grows between teacher and student, a dialogue of questions and answers, rawness and discipline, hopes and accomplishments. The experience teaches more than music.

On that day of my first appointment with her, Mrs. Spring invited me to sit in her living room after I finished the tuning, and we spent a few minutes getting acquainted while she wrote out my check. I had caught up a little on my lateness and could make my next appointment within a few minutes of my scheduled time. Still, I was agitated to feel so insecure in my day, rattled by my involuntary bird murder and barely confident that my work would please her. It surprised me that she did not check the tuning. I offered for her to check it, but she waved her hand and said she had listened to me play afterwards and that it sounded fine. It would do nicely, she said.

I had charged her my regular price, and as she handed me the check she observed that, if I would like, she could refer her students to me for tuning work. Her eyes twinkled at my surprised thanks, and then she suggested that in exchange for such references, I might be willing to discount her tunings. Would I be interested?

Of course, such an arrangement should have crossed my mind. But in the newness of my endeavor, both as a piano technician and as a woman in business, I had not yet discovered the inner workings of trade alliances. I was thrilled to hear her suggestion. I agreed, handing her a small stack of my business cards.

She studied the cards as we walked together toward the door.

"You know," she said, "my mother called while you were tuning just now. She's ninety."

"Oh," I said.

"She thought it was curious when I mentioned you were a woman. She'd never heard of a woman piano tuner before."

"Well, there aren't many," I agreed.

"Yes, well, she hesitated after I first mentioned my piano was being tuned by a woman. And then she said, in a kind of conspiratorial tone, 'Well, she'll probably do a better job.'"

I laughed with Mrs. Spring. It was a consolation of sorts, a joining of myself to a newly discovered clan of those who make a living from music, and an even bigger clan, a sisterhood of women who had always suffered limits now being thrown off. Within me, I felt I had reached a new stage.

5

Short Pieces

A lady called me to service her almost-new piano because she had just moved into a different house and had always heard one should have the piano tuned after moving and also because quite a few notes in the treble would not play. Her house was a fabulous spread-out affair, open and airy and fresh even though outside it was below freezing. She escorted me across immaculate cream-colored carpet toward the ornate studio upright and hovered near-by as I opened my tool case.

She described what she thought were out-of-place parts, perhaps disturbed by the movers, although she was almost certain it had played without problems just after it was moved in. I ran my fingers over the keys and confirmed that at least two octaves in the upper register would barely play.

As I opened the top lid to begin my investigation, she leaned forward with me, and we both peered into the disturbed area. Suddenly, one, then two, and then the third mouse leapt up from their elaborate nest and scrambled out and off of the piano. The woman shrieked involuntarily and jumped back as the mice, well-fed and glossy in their little brown coats, disappeared in all directions.

After a brief moment I poked around in the nest with my screwdriver to be sure there were no more, and once the woman had composed herself, she and I cleaned out the nest into a hastily obtained trash bag. I tuned the piano, pointed out the parts that were damaged or missing as a result of mouse gnawing, estimated repair costs, and left her with instructions for mouse control. She was horrified, embarrassed, and afraid to sit or sleep in her house, she told me as I was leaving. She never called me back.

Once a caller wanted to know just what I charged to tune a piano. I told her usually it was around fifty dollars. Well, she said after a short pause, that was too much. What would I charge to just tune the middle notes? After all, she went on, those were the only keys she played.

We had a major overhaul in our shop once on a 1940s upright Steinway, a wealthy family's piece that had been given to the most musical of the family, a young man in his twenties. It had been taken back by the family, however, and was now being fully restored by his older sister after the family discovered he had painted the piano in a full-color design which I thought was a pretty good facsimile of a Budweiser can.

An acquaintance of my ex-husband had four kids who wanted piano lessons. He had access to an old upright piano that belonged to his mother-in-law. The piano had sat in her house for years unused and gathering dust, so it was determined that he would fix it up, move it to his house, and use it for the kids. The man and a few buddies moved the piano onto his mother-in-law's carport, where I came to assist him in some major structural work and to pick up the action mechanism in order to work on it at my shop.

After many hours of labor by the man, following my directions for reattaching the legs properly and rebuilding the bottom, we were ready to reassemble the instrument. I worked several more hours, adjusting the keys and raising the pitch. In the end, he had paid me around two hundred fifty dollars and had saved himself close to another two hundred fifty by working on it himself. It was ready to take to his house.

He called me the next weekend. His voice sounded strained as he asked me if I would like to buy the piano from him for parts. It confused me for a minute, and I guess I hesitated. He then went on to explain that he had loaded the piano in his pickup to take to his house and when he went around the corner it fell off the truck, landed in the road and was in approximately twelve pieces.

I was sorry to say it, but I had no use for the parts. It had never occurred to me that he would move it without tying it down.

A lady called me one time and wanted me to come look at her piano. She had just brought it proudly home in the back of her pickup truck and, with the help of a few burly neighbors, had wrestled it into the chosen spot in her living room. She explained to me that she'd found it at a garage sale across town for only fifty dollars, and it was playing great before she moved it. But now she couldn't get it to play hardly at all and wanted me to come see what moving it had done to mess it up. She went on to say that since it had been so filthy she had stopped by a car wash when she had it loaded in her truck so she could wash it, and that it really cleaned up nice. Did I think that would have messed it up?

A friend of mine wanted a piano, but she couldn't afford to buy one. Her husband played guitar and thought a piano would be nice for their kids, but he didn't see how they would have the money. I told them it would take from $500 to $1000 to buy a fairly decent and not quite worn-out instrument. They asked if I would keep an eye out, so I agreed that if a bargain came up, I would let them know.

Not too long afterwards, I was called by a woman who was moving and wanted to know if I would haul off an old piano she had temporarily moved onto her carport the week before. Unfortunately, a big storm had flooded her area and put about six inches of water across her carport floor. The piano had taken the water for nearly twelve hours before the mini-flood subsided. She didn't expect to sell it, she said, but would let me have it to just haul it off.

I went to look at the piano and discovered that it was not really a total loss. It would take some cleaning up, but it was worth it. I called my friend and explained the situation. I didn't want it, but they could haul it off for the lady and get a piano at the same time. I would coach my friends through the clean-up, fix-up process, and they would get a more or less free piano.

So her husband rounded up a few buddies and took their flatbed truck and loaded the piano. It lay down on its back for the twenty-two-mile drive to their farm, but after it was moved into their back room my friend called to let me know it was still in good shape, all keys working. I made a date for the following weekend with my friend to come out and show her how to get started on clean up.

I arrived at her house and had barely picked up my tool case from the back seat of my car when she came out toward me. She was so excited. She explained hurriedly that her husband had already started on the fix-up work, and she wanted me to show her what to do next. Together they had figured out how to take out the action mechanism and the keys, and he had gone ahead and taken all the strings off.

It took a few seconds for that last bit of information to sink in. Took off the strings? Two hundred and fifty or more strings, each of graduated size? Strings that have to go through little guide posts and each have a careful three-wind coil made on each of the tuning pins? Those strings?

Her expression quickly changed as she watched my face. I must have looked shocked. She quickly asked what was the matter, that her husband had said strings that old wouldn't be any good and we could put on another set.

In my mind I could understand the reasoning. Guitar-player reasoning. On a guitar, you can buy a set of strings and put them on in fifteen minutes. There are six strings on a guitar. But on a piano, strings don't change unless it's a major rebuilding job, since such work involves a tremendous investment in new strings and labor, which I couldn't do for free and couldn't easily instruct them. I just looked at her. The piano sat there for a few more weeks, and was finally thrown down the hillside on the back of their eighty acres.

The guy on the phone took forever to finally tell me what his problem was. Oh, at first he had plenty to say. He had piano damage. He needed an estimate on what the repairs would cost. I asked him if it was cabinet damage, or if the damage was internal, since for cabinet damage I might send my refinishing man. Well, he paused, it was hard to explain. He paused some more. He wasn't sure. Another pause. Maybe it would be both.

Finally, he said he hoped he wouldn't offend me but he thought he should tell me what really happened. There was a long pause. He was sleeping, he said, and didn't have the door to his room completely shut. I guessed it was one of those college situations where four or five guys rent a house and share expenses. Anyway, he said he woke up in the middle of the night because someone had come into his room muttering and swearing. He could tell they were really drunk. It took him a minute to figure out what was going on, that this inebriated person was urinating on his piano.

I declined to go on that job. On the phone I told him it was probably a matter of cleaning it up, but he would need to find someone else. Sorry.

A woman named Louise called me about her old piano. It had been in the house when they moved in, she said, and she wanted to fix it up and sell it. Right away I could see there was some questionable thinking, since at the best an old upright fixed up by owners might bring in five hundred dollars, but more often a hundred or less. But rather than go into a lengthy explanation over the phone, when in fact I did not know what she had, I made an appointment to go look at the piano.

I was surprised after inspecting the frame, action, and the keys that the instrument was slightly better than average and might actually bring close to five hundred dollars if cleaned up. This was the good news. The bad news was that it had been painted, which usually ruins a piano's value. Stripping off a coat of paint required many hours of nasty, noxious work and if done at my shop would have cost a minimum of fifteen hundred dollars.

Louise, however, took this news in stride. She was home all day every day with little kids, anyway, she said, and she wanted to refinish it. If she could get five hundred dollars when her work was complete, then she would be glad. She wasn't interested in the alternative of putting on another coat of paint, which would have been less trouble but would have knocked off probably two hundred dollars from what she might get for it.

So I spent an hour, which she paid for, telling her exactly what products to buy and how to proceed. She asked about her ideas, like using tung oil to finish the wood once it was cleaned, and she agreed not to resort to desperate measures, such as turning a belt sander onto the large panels. She wrote down a list of things to remember.

Several weeks went by and then I got a call from Louise. She was having a problem and wondered if I could help. She had stripped off four distinct layers of paint, first the ugly brown, then green then pink then white, before finally getting down to the wood. Some of the wood had cleaned up nicely, she went on, but other pieces wouldn't, and she didn't know why.

From her explanation of the problem, I wasn't sure what was going on. She described a kind of sticky substance that wouldn't come off the wood even after repeated coats of stripper. She wanted to know if she could use a sander. I explained to her than sanders go right through the thin layer of veneer and can ruin a piano in just a few seconds. If it truly needed sanding, it would have to be light hand sanding only.

I came by the next afternoon. She had the piano spread out on plastic sheeting and newspapers in her dining room, panels here and there in various stages of refinishing. Her equipment was tidily contained in a carrying tray, and I could see right away that she had pursued this project with careful consideration. I praised her work and her progress, and she happily showed me several smaller pieces that had cleaned down to a beautiful walnut grain.

The top lid was a major problem, however, as was the front panel. Both were laid out on newspaper and as I examined them I was listening to her explain how she had repeatedly used stripper and only a milky paste had come off. The wood itself looked like it had been spread over with a thick coat of wood putty. The more I messed with it, the more I realized that wood putty was exactly what it was.

Worse, I began to see distinct circular patterns etched into the wood, not quite disguised by the putty. I checked over the whole surface of both large panels and the evidence became more clear. Someone had used a circular sander on this piano, I told Louise, and had cut through the veneer and then used wood putty to smooth it over before painting it.

The horrible truth was that all her work had been for nothing. There was no way to correct the damage done and no way for us to have known before all her hours of stripping off paint that underneath would not be wide panels of rich walnut, but, instead, this legacy of butchery. She was, of course, not happy to hear me tell her that the only thing she could do to make the piano look decent was to paint it.

6

People Who Have Too Much Money

*D*on't get me wrong, please. Lots of the people whose pianos I service are neither too rich nor too poor. The extremes just attract more attention.

Many of the homes I visit are average homes with clean pianos that simply need to be tuned. Any of these people would make interesting stories, too, like the men who live compromised lives after divorce and child support but still need a little Chopin in the evenings, or the couples who make do with one income so the other person can be at home to take care of the children. There are middle-aged women who live alone and keep up with local politics and plant flowers in their yards in the spring. And there are young people, single or married, with sparsely furnished homes and posters of strange art, whose pianos were brought from their childhood homes to start the new household.

I pet the dogs and play with the cats of families whose homes are cluttered with the friendly, warm smells and sounds of growing children, chili in the microwave and *Thompson Book I* on the piano. I know the houses along the streets of these towns, the schools, the churches, the bars, and performance halls. I know houses in the countryside, where the rivers run clear and where dirt roads climb steep, rocky hillsides and drop down through thick, green woods.

These things feel familiar to me, and the course of my daily work centers on these well-traveled scenes. There is, however, a less common job that crops up now and then, and draws my anxious attention. That job is when I work on a piano in a house that belongs to someone I consider excessively rich.

Among these, I went to a house once that was centered in a huge open piece of flat land, with the entire acreage surrounded by a black wrought-iron fence. Tall poplar trees lined the long cement drive that ran from the gate up to the house, and vast sculptured gardens ranged in various placements around the house and drive. Thick plantings of exotic shrubbery were ornamented by clusters of dark purple and red flowers, tapering down to glossy ivy that covered the ground under special statuary or thriving topiary.

The house was like a palace, built in two stories of massive blocks of cut gray stone with three wings that centered on a main hall, all roofed in what must have been slate, dully gleaming gray-blue in the bright summer sun. The drive circled around a large fountain that was ringed with rows of more red-flowering plants and dark green ivy, bringing me to the wide steps that led up to the towering white door. There was some doubt in my mind whether I would even be received at the front door, and I worried as I rang the bell that someone, perhaps in uniform, would come and in hushed tones tell me to please move my humble car and self to the servant's entrance around to the east side — not that I saw any such entrance, but rather imagined it as I stood in the hot sun entranced by the aroma of the nearby gardenia that flourished in tall marble planters on either side of the door.

The door was opened by a friendly woman in work clothes, clearly someone other than the actual mistress of this house. I stepped carefully onto the green marble floor, scarcely able to absorb the scene: nearby tables with legs carved in the shapes of gargoyles, their tops laden with enormous pottery vases that held fresh blooms of red hibiscus, violet asters, flaming sprays of purple and orange bird-of-paradise. My eyes peered back at me from an enormous mirror that stretched from the floor to well above my head, framed in a heavy ornate gilded frame, and I regretted not being able to just stand there for a few moments to take in every detail of the tapestries and oil paintings hanging on the high walls.

She led me down a hallway, her steps and mine echoing on the glossy marble slabs. The walls were lined with more art, each hosting its own light as though in a fine art gallery. Watercolors of Mediterranean hillsides, whitewashed villas with red tile roofs; a rosy-cheeked child in burgundy velvet, sitting by a white dappled greyhound in lustrous oil color; more scenes of countryside, shaded groves of trees with blue sky and flouncing white clouds, distant mountains; a sunset barely visible in the thick overcast threat of storm over angry waves. The scent of gardenia lingered.

We moved into an adjoining room, with me following a few steps behind the woman who made small talk about the warm weather as we walked. Our steps quieted as we entered the living room area, sinking deeply in pale pink carpet which provided a gentle glow to the whole room. The glossy black Steinway, its lid up in concert position, sat off to the side. She led me carefully past the room's furnishings: two matching couches upholstered in rose-colored silk, end tables and coffee table in mahogany and glass, a long side table with lion heads carved into the rosewood legs, its top gleaming in high polish to reflect a collection of snuff boxes, each one enameled or jeweled or framed in brass or gold.

I made psychological space for myself at the piano, shutting out my great sense of wonder at the riches around me. She helped me remove a small lamp of dangling crystals from the music desk and then left me to my work, and I began to relax as I spread out my tools and began. The tuning would not require a great effort, since the piano was in fairly good condition. With no one in the room, I was free to look around as I tuned.

The tall windows of the spacious room were curtained with deep pink velvet draperies that were generously cut to bunch up slightly on the pale carpet, tied back in thick folds by braided cord that tasseled in long silky strands beyond the wide knots at the ends. A fireplace built of the same huge blocks of cut gray stone as the outside of the house took up a wide section of the north wall, medieval in its yawning mouth where logs as long and thick as a man's body could readily burn. The hearth spread into the room with more gray stone, polished and laid flat to meet the wood flooring that formed a small arena around it. The high white mantle hosted two-feet-tall soldiers carved in marbled burgundy stone, garbed in ancient Oriental dress that reminded me of Genghis Khan, and a tall brass urn, slightly battered, that likely had been retrieved from a grave of some such ancient time as that of the Khans.

I wondered, as my eyes gazed around the room, if the

people who owned this house spent much time in this room. It seemed more like a show place, a reservoir of collected art and opulent furnishings, than a place to take off the shoes and read the evening paper. More huge arrangements of intensely red and pink flowers stood on the coffee table, and I thought it would be nice to know if the mistress of the house had arranged them, or if they were organized and delivered by a florist according to some regular weekly plan.

The view out the windows lay on a wide terrace and pool, accompanied by a small pool house at the far end. A side garden of purple hibiscus and clematis and a golden raintree sheltered a shaded rest area beside the pool, where white wrought-iron chairs were made comfortable by thick white cushions, and more small fountains splashed water across the white marble legs of little boys, permanently pouring water from white marble buckets. Pink, red, and purple profusions of gloxinia, geraniums, and caladiums grew thickly around the smooth walkways.

The water in the long rectangular pool was clean and blue, reflecting the bright sky and slightly rippled by the faint July breeze. Past the pool and the distant tidy pool house was a flat expanse of close-cropped grass that led to the far fence. Only past the fence in barely discernible detail could I see the city neighborhood, a row of small houses, old oaks, parked cars. I thought it would have been more appropriate if this mansion were built on a hilltop somewhere beyond the scope of the local city, where the only intrusion in sound or sight would have been thoroughbreds in a nearby pasture or swans on a spacious pond.

I thought of other incredible houses I had visited, not that there have been so many. One was built onto a cliff at the lake, peering down past tall tree tops to the sparkling waters. There were at least four levels in that house, stepping down the rocky outcroppings of that steep hillside. Staircases with brass handrails led past a kitchen with a stainless steel chef's style stove that sat under a giant stainless steel hood in the middle of a red-tiled floor in an enormous kitchen, past an indoor pool with tinted glass walls, revealed in little glimpses as I followed someone other than the home owner to the lowest floor where the grand piano sat by a wall of thick plate-glass windows that hovered over rock ledges and peered down through wild thickets of honeysuckle, woodbine, thunderbriar, and poison ivy onto the blue-green water of the lake.

In another home of fabulous wealth, I tuned an antique pianoforte brought from Italy to fit into a sprawling collection of European art, some with the oil paints dark and cracking in tiny lines on huge canvases of hunting scenes, still life of pheasant and trout and onions and brass platters. There were actual suits of armor and long lances of iron standing in the shaded hallway that led from the heavy wooden entry door down native stone steps to a landing where three floor levels branched off in different directions.

Many of these homes are built on large reserves of land that are, for obvious reasons, marked "Posted," barring the local men from their traditional deer hunting grounds where they used to roam across the hills and valleys in pursuit of ten-point bucks. More than one "Posted" sign have multiple bullet holes in them, punctuating the painted word with heartfelt outrage at the invasion. Gone are the old deer stands, where men — neighbors, cousins, friends — would gather in November for a week or two and set up tents, build their campfires, and reaffirm their individual ability to survive without women, kitchens, television, hot showers. The deer hunting was almost incidental to the tradition of primitive survival around a roaring fire and the communion of men, but now even this is mostly gone. The deer herds grow thick in the newly posted countryside, protected by the homes and the people who don't understand the balance of men and deer that existed before they came.

I wonder if any of those who live so well are native, or if they have brought their wealth here from spoiled cities where industry and corporate conquest have laid low the beauty of that land. Musing as I do while tuning gives me time to wonder where else these absentee home owners might have houses, perhaps a vacation place in the South Pacific. I let my fantasies lead me astray as I work each string to its desired pitch, wondering whether these people ever eat spaghetti or watch the six o-clock news or if they ever worry about paying the bills.

What would they worry about, I like to guess. Maybe they have a loss on the stock market? Maybe a work of art they like is bought by someone else? Is it at all possible that they occasionally have indigestion or don't like to wake up early? What human burdens must they bear?

On that day in the room with pale pink carpet, I wondered these things again and was surprised at the end of my work that the woman of the house appeared and invited me to sit on her silk couch while she wrote me a check. I had let myself get so carried away with my imaginings it was hard to grasp that she was paying me from an ordinary checkbook instead of perhaps opening a small wooden chest and taking out gold coins or rare jewels.

She was a friendly person, her petite, trim body clad in soft, tailored cotton blouse and pants. Her smile crinkled the corners of her blue eyes, and I wanted so much to ask her where all the money came from, how it was that she and not I, nor thousands of others, could live in such extravagance. I bit my tongue. She inquired, predictably, about the condition of the piano and received my positive report. She asked if I could remind her on a yearly basis when tunings should be done, since she seemed to lose track.

There was such a human quality about her that I felt warmly toward her, surprising myself with my own urge to somehow become her friend. I was intrigued that she might actually sit in this room with her shoes off and read the evening paper. I considered the possibility that, in fact, she might have arranged the hibiscus and asters herself.

I wondered if she folded her own laundry, whether the underwear in her and her husband's dresser drawers were as neatly organized as the snuff boxes on the rosewood side table. I sensed a pride in her of accomplishment, a life's work well done, pleasure in her ease of living that permitted travel to distant seas, children sent to Ivy League colleges, and time for idle attention to manicured nails and fashionable silk suits.

Perhaps I imagined it, because I needed to make her a more sympathetic figure in my own mind, but I thought there was some undercurrent of sadness with her. Maybe a tragedy too awful to dwell on, an illness or loss she wanted to forget. Maybe it was present in her mind enough for me to get a glimmer of it because in order to forget her grief she needed to play the piano, therefore the call for my service. I would not ask, and she did not tell.

I find it mysterious that some of us stumble across such fortune, not as a result of harder work or greater intelligence or a more deserving spirit, but simply by the fate of the moment. For some, perhaps it is a birthright, but why that person born to that wealth and not some other? And how is it that in so many ways we are the same, yearning for a freshly roasted breast of chicken to eat when we are hungry or a warm, soft chocolate brownie late at night when the house is dark except for the light in the refrigerator as we get a glass of cold milk? Yet here they are, the few without worry over the monthly bills to pay, a Mercedes or Jaguar to drive, houses that carry every conceivable comfort and exotic luxury, simply by the fortune of being cast in the weave of the fabric of life where the spindle piles up a cluster of golden threads in one lucky spot, leaving the next few throws of the loom unevenly bare and plain.

Folks Who Don't Have Enough Money

*T*he woman's voice on the phone was faint, not because the phone line was bad but more as if she languished in an exaggerated role of female passivity. I strained to hear her over the noise coming from the back of my shop where the refinishing man was putting another coat of lacquer on a turn-of-the-century grand, a combination of spraying hiss and the steady roar of the air compressor. Finally I had to carry the phone around the end of my desk and stand on the porch to hear.

Her husband had brought her a piano. Her biggest concern was to find out how to put moisture back into the piano. Some of the veneer on the sides and panels was loose, and she felt sure it was because the piano was too dry.

"What else is wrong with it?" I asked.

"The keys won't play very well," she murmured, "and I think some of the felt things are bad."

"Do the keys stick?"

"Yes, they won't go down or up."

"Tell me about the felt things. Are they the parts that hit the strings?" I was rapidly forming an opinion.

"Yes, they are supposed to, but some of them are loose, and they don't move." She went on to describe the lovely engraving on the front panels and how she wanted to refinish it. Could I come look at it to see how much it would cost to fix?

Yes, I made an appointment. It would cost her fifteen dollars for me to drive to her house, not enough to cover my actual expense in time alone, but as much as I usually charge when I suspect I am going to deliver a death sentence to someone's fond hope. In the meantime, she promised, she was going to start to work on the cabinet.

It was a cloudy morning with a glaze of wetness over the trees and pastures. The turnoff from the highway was a familiar one, and I relaxed as the countryside spread out in front of me along the narrow county road. Just the faintest hint of transparent green was starting to fuzz up on the trees across the hillsides, maybe a little early for a normal spring, but the winter had been mild.

After about five miles along the pavement, I turned off on a dirt road which was squishy from light rain the night before. It was mountaintop land, though, and I wasn't worried about getting into deep mud. I drove along another two miles until I came to the driveway turnoff, marked as she had described by a large faded-red sign hand painted in black letters with "No Trespassing." The drive angled along the south face of the hillside, dropping steadily as it proceeded first toward the west, then the south, then west again.

A young deer stopped my progress at one point, standing in the driveway, staring at me. It was in a sharp cut of land, with a wide ravine coming down on the left from the outbreak of limestone at the top, a massive line of gray boulders that jagged in and out along the crest of the hill. The natural stands of oak and hickory populated the rocky slope, mostly mature trees whose brown and gray bark served to hide the rest of the deer from my first glances. But I knew they were there.

I came to a full stop about twenty feet away as the yearling doe gave me her full attention. I studied the nearby land and soon found three more young ones and two does, standing in a loose group on the edges of the ravine. Then she bolted out of the road, leaping in long bounds over big rocks, a fallen tree, and a side crevasse of the ravine to regain the companionship of the others. I let off my brake and the car eased down the lane.

The road followed between the curve of the higher bluff land on the right and the ravine and its bluffs on the left. I had been over a half mile so far. The gray rocks peppered the hillside as it funneled into the ravine, each of them covered in mosses of the most brilliant lime, olive, and palest white-green. The emerald grasses, bushes, and tree leaves that would come in another month would overcome this garb of fragile green, but for this time, the rocks gave the hillside color that sparkled against the grays, browns, and blacks of the tree trunks, fallen leaves, and dirt.

About a quarter mile passed as I followed the road alongside the ravine, until it opened into a large pond. Just past the pond sat several abandoned vehicles scattered beside the driveway, and then there was the house. It was a trailer house (excuse me, "mobile home") with a porch, carport, and extra room built onto the side of it. Three vehicles sat near the porch, an older model Jeep Wagoneer, a battered red and white Ford pickup, and a tan and white Chevy van, apparently the ones most roadworthy. The carport was full of junk, including several large piles of crushed beer cans, a familiar brand identified by the blue and white colors on the crinkled aluminum.

I parked close to the porch and by the time I had carried my tools to the door, it was opened by a woman carrying a small child on her hip. Her stringy brown hair kept falling across her face as she led me through the narrow trailer's living room to an adjoining room, added onto the side of the trailer in rough construction with open two-by-four studs and an uneven floor. The piano leaned slightly toward me as I stood in front of it, causing me some concern that it might suddenly drop through the stained plywood to the rocky ground underneath.

Four young children — all under the age of ten as best I could guess — gathered nearby as I opened the cabinet. They, like their mother and baby sibling, were dressed in unmatched, worn-out and wrinkled clothing that seemed dirty. Only one had on shoes on that cold and wet early spring day, but the trailer and room were overly warm from the big wood stove that sat near the gun rack in the larger room. There were at least six guns, shotguns and rifles, on the rack and several bill caps at various stages of wear: a black one with gold lettering that said "Caterpillar," a blue one with "Ford" on it, a faded gray one with a replica of the Confederate flag stitched across the front.

The piano keys were sitting in a jumbled assortment of heights, most of them immovable as I pressed on them. Many of the ivories were missing, leaving a hopscotch effect of brown wood, black keys, and the occasional white. At that point I knew the piano was hopeless, but I went ahead and removed the rest of the panels, more of a courtesy to the anxious woman than anything else. Besides, it would be useful to be able to show her all the reasons why this instrument was a lost cause.

As I pointed my flashlight at the tuning pins and strings, thickly coated with rust, and at the hammers, many of which had come unglued and now looked like dingy seagulls frozen in perpetual flight toward open water, the woman explained how she had paid only twenty-five dollars for it, how it took five of their strong friends to get it loaded on their pickup and moved into this room.

Where had it been? I asked her, not surprised when she described a dirt-floor shed that was open on its south side. The piano had probably shared its storage facilities with a horse, bales of hay, rusting 1930s farm equipment, and empty moonshine jugs. I sympathetically pointed out all the reasons why the piano was worthless, holding my line even as the woman fought with the reality, gently arguing to me that she could clean it up herself, that the wood she had already cleaned and oiled on one panel looked a lot better.

Finally, it was inevitable that I had to spell it out, stating to her that it would take more money to fix this piano than it would take to buy a better one, and that even after spending the money it would not be a worthy instrument. Too many years of exposure to the elements, probably at some point even standing outside in rain, had left this piano with only one final remedy. Anticipating her thought, I said it didn't even have value for parts.

I charged her fifteen dollars, which she paid in an odd silence, the children drifting off to some tiny back room where the television continued its chatty noise. As I eased my car over the chuckholes and rocks in the drive, once again past the Thunderbird with its front doors off and leaning against a nearby oak, past the Impala with its hood off and the hood brackets sticking up in the air like thin, mechanical arms, past the three pickup trucks, or what was left of them, one with only the bed and rear axle sitting alone with its vibrant turquoise paint job partially camouflaged by tall brown grass and weeds that had grown up around it in past summers.

There was no sign that this poverty had been a choice. There were no crystals hanging in the window to catch the sunlight, no peace signs carved in thick walnut hanging on the wall. There was no garden where herbs and tomatoes and okra might accompany a few marijuana plants, nor was there a comfortable sense of acceptance of borderline living in the mood of the house. Instead, there was a despair based on hunger and not just hunger for food, although I felt there must have been that as well.

I pondered the beauty of their land and how the trailer was positioned so that from the porch they could look out across a narrow valley toward distant blue mountains, how each drive to town was a journey past bluffs and jutting gray limestone and oak trees with crooked limbs that stood black against the sky. I questioned whether another piano would ever come here, or if that 1919 Crown Upright Grand would stand there on the sagging plywood floor, like the doorless Thunderbird between the oaks, until these people lived no more.

Once a woman called me to appraise her piano, which she said she wanted to sell. As I drove toward her house on the day of the appointment, I wondered what I would find. The address was about twenty miles out of town, along a road that I knew was not known for its high-value real estate. At the turnoff onto the county road, I realized it was a road not often traveled, since it dropped off at a sharp angle from the pavement and quickly narrowed to a width that defined it. Within the directed eight-tenths of a mile, however, I arrived at what was the correct house.

There were three outbuildings, one of them surrounded with truck cabs, trucks of "semi" size. There were at least five truck cabs, some so old it took me back to my young girl days in the 1950s when I'd travel with my parents and younger sister over the mountains on Highway 71 from Ft. Smith to Fayetteville to see my mother's family, when parts of the road were so narrow that someone had to pull over to let the others come by, when the road was so treacherous that when storms came or fog rolled up from the valleys, cars would creep along at fifteen miles per hour, and my father would curse and dodge semi-trucks that suddenly appeared in front of us on the steep, foggy curves.

I drove to the end of the big circular drive, arriving at the steps to the door of the house. It was an ancient log cabin, a place that may have been there in this wooded under-hill cove since the Civil War, at least since the 1880s when the railroad first came through this area. I wondered if the piano had been new at about the same time.

I stood at the door in the cold through three knockings because I knew someone was home. I could hear the television. I saw smoke coming out of the chimney. A dark blue Chevy pickup sat close beside me, the mud on its sides not yet dry. Finally the door was opened by a withered, short woman with shockingly black hair that seemed to stick out in odd straight clumps from all over her head. Her face was pasty white, and her black watery eyes and naturally red lips seemed like makeup for Halloween. She motioned me inside urgently, as though she had waited for me a long time. Her voice of greeting was melodious and warm, incongruous with the face.

She led me past a blazing-hot wood-burning stove to a small upright piano that sat a mere six feet from the stove. It was beautifully carved on the front and legs, careful workmanship that was the trademark of Victorian furniture. Each fleur-de-lis was cut and smoothed by hand, each tendril of the vine that draped across the burled walnut front shaped slowly and lovingly by a worker who admired what he did every day. The legs were shapely, like a Rubens woman, with dipping curves and circles carved into thick chunks of virgin walnut stock. I wondered if there would ever again be a day when furniture makers could afford to cut four-inch-thick pieces of walnut into slabs fifteen inches wide and two feet tall, to have it carved out in designs and curls so rich. I wondered if there would ever be a day when such walnut trees were again available, growing slowly and stately in well-drained, rich soil.

I played up and down the keyboard, noting wildly out-of-tune notes at frequent intervals. I opened the top and took off the front panel, seeing immediately that the hammers were doing the extreme wobbling routine that signals major mechanical failure of the action. The tuning pins had been driven into the pinblock a long time ago, as far as I could tell. The strings' coils on the pins were embedded in the wood of the pinblock in some places, clearly as deep as they could ever go. The pinblock wood was fractured on the surface in tiny dark lines. When I put my tuning hammer on a pin to check the torque, it moved just under the weight of the hammer. The piano was a basket case, a bushel of bolts. It was worn out and cooked.

She told me she got this piano from her grandmother, who brought it from Kansas City when she got married. She told me she had played it all her life, that it had been her mother's piano for a while. It had always stayed in this house, where she had been born, too. She told me she had to sell it now because her thirty-year-old son was in jail, and she needed bail money.

I was comfortable in the little living room, looking for a second and even third time at her worthless piano. I tried to think up things I could tell her that would make it better. I looked at the peculiar blonde oak coffee table, obtusely square and fifties in design, with its assortment of household life: a stack of mail, an assortment of prescription bottles, an ashtray spilling over with butts, a pair of dirty leather gloves, a can of Coke, two plastic pots of poinsettia from Wal-Mart, losing leaves and still marked with the chartreuse sale stickers.

There was no way around it. I told her the truth. The piano was worthless, unless she could find someone who would value the walnut cabinet. I gave her the name of a man I knew who did specialty cabinet work. I had never asked him, but maybe he would want the cabinet to gut and turn into a desk or liquor cabinet or bookshelves. It was a long shot.

She was not surprised. She had been afraid it would be something like that. She only needed two hundred dollars. Would I give her two hundred dollars to just take it?

No, I couldn't do it. I had rafters in my shop full of pianos that had died similar deaths, kickboards and top lids and front panels and ornately carved legs in walnut, mahogany, oak. There was no future in it, no profit for me or my dad when we finally might one day have a customer who needed a panel that ours would fit, or could be cut down to size for. The cost of rent for the space alone made it a ludicrous proposition. Still, I considered it. Would my cost be worth her need?

No, I couldn't do it. I told her. No.

She took out her checkbook to pay me my appraisal fee, out here, twenty dollars. I hated taking the money, but I'm not a charity. I have to remind myself.

I pulled my coat around me as I stepped out her door onto the steep wooden steps down to the ground beside my car. She apologized to me for bringing me all this way for a worn-out piano. I told her to give that carpenter a call. I never wanted to know what he said, but I was ninety percent sure he said "no."

I meet lots of good people who choose to have no money. Somewhere back down the line, probably in the sixties or early seventies, they decided the world had it all wrong, and they weren't buying it. They are lucky to be able to give themselves up to a life of deprivation that seems harsh to me. I want Ziploc bags and hot running water. For them, these are not necessary. There are not many so pure.

Once, I went on a call to tune a piano that belonged to a man who lived in a bus. The bus was wheelless, and its axles sat on big rocks in the middle of a wooded wilderness. He wasn't there alone, but rather was one of a group who communally owned the rough land, who struggled with bugs and drought and Johnson grass to grow fresh onions, garlic, green beans, marigolds, and gladioli that they could sell at local natural foods stores or farmers' markets. One of the group lived in a teepee made of long slim poles — probably cut from river-bottom sycamore — and what she described as a parachute that wrapped over the high poles and formed a wonderful funnel that opened down to the packed-hard ground where her possessions and bed sat on the dirt. I was invited inside to see what it was like, and it was an intriguing mix: ancient shape rising up to a tiny clear hole at the top where her fire's smoke went out, the lower circumference spacious for stacks of modern things like jeans and flannel shirts and a modern chair. I thought that if I sat there on that chair my mind would twist into a strange configuration of peyote vision and milk crate shelves.

The piano the man had was at the very back of the bus. It was a nasty little spinet that multiple generations of mice had called home. The entire cabinet had been painted psychedelic yellow with orange swirls and purple peace signs, bright green, clumsy marijuana leaves, and various slogans like "Be Here Now." I made him dig out the nests as I lifted the keys, not anxious to find my fingers bitten by current residents of the fetid castles built of chewed hammer felts, bridle straps, and key wood. Interestingly, the pitch was not far from standard A-440, and the tuning progressed reasonably.

I accepted payment of some money and the balance in produce from their gardens. I took a bushel of organically grown tomatoes and another bushel of green beans, which I wanted to can over the upcoming weekend, in lieu of my own crop which had not been properly planted, not been properly weeded, and since been chewed to the ground by an overpopulation of deer.

It was an old school bus, I noted as I stepped down from the front door. I had passed by his meager stack of clothing, the amazingly blatant metal tray where marijuana stems and seeds sat forlorn on the tin surface. I had passed a small kerosene cook stove, mounted where two seats would have been, and a plywood table large enough to serve two. It seemed a comfortable home, a place where one could read late at night by kerosene lamp interrupted only by the crickets and bright-eyed mice slipping in to chew even more of the piano.

About a year later a friend told me that this man had to sell his piano to post bond to get out of jail. It seems a large crop of ragweed grown for its value as an herb had been staked out by local law enforcement, mistaken as a marijuana crop. There is evidently some similarity in the two plants' appearances.

When the SWAT team descended and froze everyone spread-eagle up against their teepees and trailers and huts and bus to be felt over for weapons and contraband, this guy was found to be in possession of a half-ounce of marijuana. They busted him, frustrated that the big field of marijuana they had watched for two weeks, flown over with military helicopters and brought down with five sheriff's deputies' vehicles, two state troopers, and the local DEA guys had turned out to be ragweed.

He sold his piano, lucky to find sympathetic buyers who paid him five hundred dollars for the still-vital Acrosonic so he could post bond. He never served time, simply slapped as many have been for refusing the sheet-rock house and nine-to-five. Whoever bought his psychedelic spinet never called me.

Driving

I have an intimate relationship with my car. I feel the grainy texture of the pavement against the bottom of my feet as though my nerve endings somehow ran through to the tires. When I'm driving along and a tire hits a chuckhole or a piece of lumber lying there on the road, the impact occurs throughout my body, as if someone had shoved me. I feel the car. It is an extension of my body and my will.

I believe that if you inhabit your car as if it were a larger body to exist in, it will do things for you that it normally would not do. For example, I get flats, but not when it would make me late or when it is raining. Instead, it is a quiet Saturday morning. After a leisurely sleep-in and a slow hot shower, I glance out the window and there is the flat. Right rear, like a pancake. Right down to the rim. But it's okay, because I have time to put on the doughnut spare and take it for repairs.

My car senses things that I somehow miss. Like yesterday, I was backing up in a parking lot and carefully looked all around before maneuvering backward. At almost the full apex of my rear swing, I realized there was a large, battered truck sitting directly behind where I had been. Somehow I had not seen it, but my car had and managed to turn just inches this side of its big, square, rusted metal front bumper. I had a similar experience last week, missing a trash dumpster by just a hair.

In those situations, there is no principle of basic physics or statistics that would produce anything less than a fifty percent chance that I would hit the obstacle. So far, I've hit nothing. Maybe a day will come when I hit cars, trash bins, and the side of my garage, thus producing the other fifty percent. I suggest that that day will only come when and if I am driving a car with which I have no relationship.

My car and I spend a lot of time together, traveling a thirty-minute drive from home to town every day, first to drop off a kid at school, then to my shop/office to get geared up for the day's appointments. Then I'm off, driving across town, to the next town or out into the countryside to the pianos of the day.

The secret adventures I have with my car are sometimes so exciting that I have to talk with the car about them. Once I had an appointment in a rough area in the southwestern part of the county. There was a narrow paved road that went about six miles south from the nearest main road. Then off this little road was a dirt road that turned west and one that turned east. I had gone up the west road as it wound up a steep, rocky hill that had washed out across the road in several places, then past a little farm on the left and then a spring on the right. After another half mile of curving up and around the north face of that hill, I came to the top at a T intersection, where I turned left and drove along a straight, flat stretch of road before coming to the farm where my job was. As it turned out, the people had forgotten I was coming and had failed to leave their house unlocked. Not knowing this, of course, and after giving them fifteen minutes to show up, I decided to use my extra time before the next appointment to do some exploring.

I dragged out my official county map. I knew my next job was on a road that ran parallel to the first narrow road I had been on, another old trail that had been used so long it had finally received a coat of asphalt. There weren't shoulders, curbs, or anything else that makes a road, just asphalt on the old dirt bed. I figured there had to be some cut-through road that connected the two, which would save me lots of miles of driving north, then a little bit east, and then all the way back down south again.

Slipping back down that steep, rocky hill I had first turned west on, I contemplated the road facing me, the one that turned east off the pavement. It was just as steep and it seemed not so well traveled, but according to the map it did in fact connect with the other road where I wanted to go. It was a very thin line on the map, and I suspected that there might be some rough going before I got all the way across it, but I figured I could make it. I'd been in rough spots before.

Any dirt back road in the Ozarks is at its worst in the middle (unless its a dead-end road) because folks who live on that road want to take the quickest route to the nearest paved road. So half go one way and the other half go the other, and the middle of the road hardly gets used. I figured that I'd be about two miles in when this road would get bad.

I drove past a few nice homes, several large, modern chicken houses, old falling-down barns, sheet metal sheds, rusting 1950s pickup trucks, and ancient farm equipment, spaced at decent intervals along the verdant pasture land. Willow and sycamore clustered around serene old ponds whose waters rose up cold and sweet from year-round springs. I could see across the flat land to other hilltops blue in the distance.

The soil is shallow in most places of Ozark hilltop, washed away over the decades of use as pasture, robbed of its renewal when the trees were cut down and the annual blanket of falling leaves could no longer nourish the soil. Along this long flat stretch, flinty fist-sized rocks had cropped up on the surface like an annual growth of strawberries, and the farmers on their tractors had dragged their large hooked rakes across their pastures to gather the rock crop and pile it up along the edges of their fields or in sharp draws to protect the land there from eroding.

The fences had suffered from the shallowness of the land, their postholes abortively shortened when the digger hit solid rock. In such cases, the framer will stand with a long iron pole, pointed at one end, and drive it down against the stubborn layers of sandstone, shattering off pieces until enough depth is gained to hold the post securely. Or, ingeniously, and especially on corners, he might build a wide cylinder out of multiple layers of hog wire and fill it with the abundant resource, rocks, until it stands mightily in its own weight and holds the straining force of the long, tight length of fence wire. Along the run of the fences, cedar had sprung up, and blackberry vines and young locust formed a line of vegetation that housed cardinals and mockingbirds. Dense clusters of grass edged the taller growth, home to field mice, voles, shrews, and a five-lined skink whose iridescent blue markings flashed at me as he escaped back into his miniature thicket.

After about a mile and a half, the land heaved up into sharp angles, pasture giving way to rougher tracts of rock and woods. The road narrowed considerably, past what I guessed must have been the last large chicken farm along this stretch. Up to this point, chicken trucks and feed trucks and fuel trucks had to go frequently, even when the weather was bad, and so the roads had to be good.

The narrower stretch was still used, though. I could see clear evidence of regular usage in the muddy driving tracks. The mud holes were bigger, and after about a quarter mile I came to one mud hole that went beyond my normal description of being even a pondette. This thing stretched from the front bumper of my now-nervous Nissan station wagon on and on, with an ugly, long, high center of grassy mud, for a distance of at least twenty feet. It was a lake.

I had to drive through it, though, because I was having an adventure, and this was my chosen route. Nothing would stop me. I turned off the air conditioner and rolled down the window so I could hear immediately if I started to drag center. I slowly eased the car into the opaque brown water. The grass growing alongside the muddy lake was tall and lush, entangled with little flowers and vines, and it brushed my elbow as the car slid along the deepening water.

It occurred to me that I shouldn't let my speed get too low, because it was likely that the ground I would soon reach in the middle of this puddle stayed wet a lot and probably wasn't very firm. However, I couldn't risk going so fast that I would scrape underneath. I pulled my elbow away from the distraction of the lazy grass and focused on driving. Keep up the speed, steer carefully. Perhaps drive just a hair to the right, get the tires up out of the ruts just a bit but not far enough to where my right fender would be scratched by the three-year old saplings growing close on the edge of the track. The grass that was thriving so richly in the middle of the road between the two tracks made brushing sounds as it rubbed underneath the belly of my car.

Luckily, the Ozark rock was steady along the roadbed, and no big reservoirs of mud sank my tires below the critical level. The car never dragged center, and I was soon picking up my speed as I emerged from the lake. The water streamed off my car's lower body and wheels as I continued along the road. The knees and shoulders of pale gray rock giants stuck up here and there in the roadway, but if I slowly crawled across them, none of them bumped into me.

The land seemed to be rising slightly. The forest along the left side of the road started to thin out, and I could see the massive outcroppings of rock rising sideways out of the mountain as it reached its plateau. To my right, the land started to narrow, and I could see through the early summer growth enough to glimpse a steep drop-off into a deep green ravine. Old grapevines traversed the gaps between the tall trunks in an understory that met the tops of redbuds, cedars, and saplings. I don't like heights, and my gut had a sudden height-panic reaction to the sheer pitch of the hillside I now found myself on.

I knew I was close to the halfway point, since I hadn't passed any houses in some time. I figured the worst was probably over. If I just stayed with this narrow, rutted, rock-riddled pathetic excuse for a road, surely soon I would pass the next house, and the road would improve. I steered carefully around another outcrop of boulders, narrowly missing a leaning locust tree that was positioned in devilish counterpoint to a particularly pointed jag of limestone. The road curved sharply to the left, and I faced the car uphill, where the road approached the top of the slope. It was at that moment, with the back of my car now positioned just twenty feet from the drop-off into the deep green ravine, that I saw the gate.

It was a standard, galvanized, gray metal stock gate, three horizontal bars fastened to an upright bar on either end, with a strong diagonal bar that reinforced it all. The chain that looped through one upright bar and around an impressive treated timber post was a heavy logging chain and the padlock, similarly, was big and heavy-looking. I didn't bother to get out of the car to examine the gate or the lock. There was no house, barn, or other sign of life nearby — not even cows. I could see fifty yards of road beyond the gate, where it passed through the last of the boulders and crested the hill, trees close on either side. The curve just behind me was chipped from the limestone hillside, then the hill dropped down to the bottom of the ravine, probably three hundred yards of ferns, mosses, and oak trees that grew out of the ground at a thirty-degree angle.

There was no place to turn around. No widening or flattening of the roadside. I had to back up. I talked with my car. We moved slowly backwards. The curve was negotiated, even though every tendon in my body was screaming under the pressure of remaining calm, remaining calm, even though all my rearview mirrors showed me the blackening space of dark green where it fell into the chasm behind me. The car got me through. It gently backed up, responded through the miracle of steering without leaping capriciously off the edge of the hillside. It backed up as I talked to it, the tires following the track of the road as the muddy, rocky trail turned slowly back to run parallel with the ridge of the mountaintop. I slowly relaxed as the precipitous curve moved farther in front of my receding car, focusing now on my backwards progress, perhaps to find some widening or flattening sufficient for a turnaround.

I gave my best assistance to the car as it maneuvered backwards over the shoulders and knees of the gray giants, sure that they were shaking in laughter at my retreat after my previous proud progress. They had me again; there was no escape. The lake loomed in my short-term memory.

I refused to be afraid. I'd made it in. I would make it out. Me and the car. The sweet scent of crushed grass rose fresh in my nose, and pale green leaves mixed with the dark olive cedars and the emerald grass like strong liqueur, like smooth tequila as it curls around before it rolls down the back of the throat. I would enjoy this, perversely.

After several more yards of careful backing up, I found a spot where the hill's slope to the east was only slight, and I braved the few protruding rocks — with verbal assurances to my car's rear end and exhaust system — to force the back end up the slope enough to give my front end some maneuvering room toward the right side of the road. The front bumper gently bent a cluster of young sumac as I put the car in drive gear for a foot's progress. I backed up the rocky slope again, the engine pushing the back tires up out of the entrenched rut and onto the greenery of the slope. I nosed forward again, the saplings bending, their bark cut by the pressure of the bumper.

It took about ten, maybe twelve backward and forward maneuvers before the car was turned around. I worked up a sweat. Then it was over. It was time to drive back over land already discovered, horrors which should have been once instead of twice, blackberry vines that got to slice my paint once, but should never have had the second chance.

I had the opportunity, some months later, to let an employee in the county judge's office know that his official map of the county had a problem. He had the map on his office wall, and I pointed out the road I had taken, showed him the county road number and the track it led from the one paved road to the other. I didn't go into detail about my adventure on the road. I did make it clear that there was a gate, a padlocked gate, across that county road. Wasn't that wrong, I asked? Of course, was the response. They're not supposed to do that.

I didn't ask who "they" were. Whether it was, in fact, a county road or not, I don't remember that I got an answer. My conclusion was that it was not. It was, obviously, serving as a private road, not marked as such, but clearly controlled by someone who stopped the world at that point.

My car suffered a small dent on the underside of the back bumper. One of the shoulders of those laughing giants. Laughing now no less than they have laughed since around 1800 when the first wagons and other horse-drawn contraptions have tried to pass through countryside that slows down and stops even deer. The ridges remain unmoved. The water comes, as it has for thirty thousand years, from the tops of the hills to make lakes in the roadways. The leaves grow thick and in various vital shades of what we call green, accented by the pink and white flowers of spring, the yellow of summer growth, and the rusty red of fall — the beautiful face of a primal force so potent that roads for cars or wagons remain subjective.

Artists

I was just getting ready to sit down for dinner when the call came. The stage manager at the arts center sounded tense.

"Can you come down here right away?" he asked apologetically. "The artist says there's something wrong with the piano."

Something wrong with the piano. It was anybody's guess what that meant.

"Did she say what exactly was wrong?" I asked wearily. I had planned to go the evening performance, which started in a hour and a half, enough time for a dinner with wine (of which I had already had a glass) and a shower and getting dressed in nice clothes. I had looked forward to this, an evening just for me, relaxed and quiet for the symphony and Beethoven on the piano.

"Something about the keys being slow," he said, helpless as the man on the street when it came to knowing pianos. "She can't get the notes to repeat, she said."

"Okay," I said, hesitantly. I'd have to dump my whole plan. "I can be there in a half hour, forty minutes at the most."

"Great," he said. "I'll tell her."

I had been at the piano just four hours earlier. There was a note on it, left by the artist from her morning rehearsal. *Key sticking in treble,* the note said. *Please do something.*

I had tuned the instrument, a Steinway nine-foot concert grand, new and in excellent condition, carefully watching for slow keys or any other kinds of problems. I found one key that didn't repeat as fast as it was supposed to, and I pulled out the action so I could adjust the repetition lever spring for a slightly faster response. I had congratulated myself for my skill and speed in accomplishing my work. The piano was excellent.

Now, as I rushed around in my sweat pants and tennis shoes, telling my daughter when to turn off the stove, what to serve herself, what time I'd be home, I was torn between ridiculing myself for failing to be thoroughly professional in concert piano preparation and being completely disgusted with the artist for nit-picking the piano to find a target for her performance nerves. I'd have to go the concert without dinner, without a shower, without dressing up. I'd have to work, under pressure and under the scrutiny of an over-wrought artist, with a glass of wine on an empty stomach. Great.

The thirty-minute drive into town was dead time, and I turned up the radio to take my mind off my stress, then turned it off in irritation. The miles crept by slowly. What could be the problem, I wondered. None of the keys were sticking earlier. It must be in her mind.

The stage manager was waiting for me in the hallway. "She's a basket case," he said softly. "I hope you can reassure her."

"I plan to."

"Even if it's not the piano," he went on, wryly.

"Exactly," I confirmed.

Orchestra members outfitted in their black dresses or tuxedos were already gathering backstage, unzipping canvas cello covers and assembling trombones. I felt shabby in my sweats and sneakers. It was intimidating to be certain that the stage lights highlighted my slightly inebriated condition, the faint glaze to my eyes, the flush in my cheeks. I had a brief mental conversation: *I still know what I need to know. This is probably a psychology job, not piano repair. We will do this and we will be fine.*

I laid my tool case down on the floor beside the piano, shut out the activity around me and started checking the keys, starting in the bass. The notes all repeated just fine. I worked my way up the keyboard, playing each note in a combination pattern, slow fast fast fast slow slow fast fast fast. Nothing. I was about two-thirds of the way up the keyboard when the artist rushed up to me. Her dark hair was carefully arranged, flowing down onto her shoulders where it rested against the blue and green floral silk dress that continued the flowing, down her arms, across her hips, below her knees. She was wringing her hands.

"This piano is terrible," she began urgently. "There are many notes that won't repeat." She began striking keys in the mid-treble area, an area I had just begun checking. Her attack on the piano was shocking. She used both hands to repeatedly strike a single key, forcing it faster and faster until the rhythm of the key's movement reminded me of a woodpecker's head rattling against a dead tree trunk.

"See what I mean?" she demanded, turning to me with a look of anger and panic on her face. "I can't perform with this instrument in this condition."

"Yes," I said carefully, "I can see there is a problem." I tried the key she had assaulted. It seemed slightly slow, but still within normal parameters. I decided to give her more room to express herself.

"Here," I said, getting up from the bench, "sit down and show me the ones that are giving you trouble."

So she sat, seemingly grateful for the opportunity to express herself, but her whole body was stiff with tension as she moved over a two- or three-octave range in the upper end of the keyboard, striking several notes with the woodpecker method, then playing snatches of music, then back to attacking the few whose lackluster response offended her.

"Here," she would say, "and this one. And this one. But this one is the worst." And she returned to the first one she had singled out for battering, a B-flat that failed her speed test. Several of the strikes she made against it with her rapid-fire fingering indeed resulted in no sound. The key was skipping. I confirmed that I understood what the problem was, explaining that there were things I could try.

She stood up then, visibly relieved that not only was there a problem, but I understood it, and I would fix it. I could tell that she needed this. I wondered if this was part of her concert prep at all of her performances. I was reassuring to her, explaining that I would go through the entire piano and make sure all the repetition was improved. She was ecstatic, and flowed off the stage toward her dressing room.

The audience would start arriving in about thirty minutes. I actually had very little I could do. No piano will repeat consistently with that kind of attack, and in that regard I was positive that this was a case of artist nerves I was dealing with. On the other hand, there was some merit to her complaint, because some of the keys she had pointed out were failing to repeat as much as they should have. I got an idea.

I turned to the stage manager, hovering nearby. "What is the status of the humidity control system?" I asked him. "Has anything changed lately?" I knew the system was computerized, so it was not a big deal to check. Normally, the building and the piano were kept at a factory-level forty-two percent relative humidity.

"Well," he began, "as a matter of fact, this morning when she was rehearsing, she complained that she was cold and demanded that we turn off the cooling system."

A light came on in my head. "Can you check the humidity for me, please?" I asked. He rushed off.

I began taking the piano apart, targeting the area of her concern with tests on the spring tension. The one B-flat was lethargic, and even when I tightened the spring, I could not gain the response I wanted. I decided to swap parts, exchanging the B-flat parts for parts from key number one, which is hardly ever played. I was just tightening the screws on the replacement part when the stage manager arrived, somewhat breathlessly, back at my side.

"You're not going to like this," he began. "The humidity is seventy-one percent."

Well, it all made sense. It had been raining. They had turned off the system so she wouldn't be cold. The wood had started absorbing moisture, and now it had progressed to this point. It would get worse, especially when the house was full of people tracking in moisture on their shoes, shaking their umbrellas, a building full of people breathing out moisture with every breath. Not a good situation.

I turned to the stage manager. "You've got to max the system right now. Get this moisture out of the air."

"But she said she couldn't be cold, or she couldn't perform properly. If we max the system, she'll be cold."

"Okay," I said. "Somebody needs to go tell her what the situation is. Let her decide if she wants the piano swimming or if she wants to be a little cold."

I continued to work, tightening repetition level springs throughout the treble. I watched the jacks move as if they were in slow motion, when in optimum conditions their movement would be crisp and instantaneous. Nothing I could do about the jacks. I turned to one of the orchestra members tuning his violin nearby.

"When is the piano part of the program?" I asked.

"After intermission," he said. "The first half is just symphony."

"Thanks."

Okay, I thought to myself. Time for drastic measures.

The stage manager came back. The artist was with him. Her eyes were big, her hands gripped tightly in front of her. I could hear people starting to take seats in the audience.

"I can't perform if I'm cold," she said, thrusting her face toward me strongly as if I was personally responsible for all her problems in life. "Can't you do anything?"

"Yes," I said pleasantly, "as a matter of fact. I'm going to try an experiment. Since you don't perform until the second half, I'm going to have the piano moved into the utility room across the hall so I can work on it longer."

She brightened immediately. "Oh, I'm so relieved. Do you think it will be in good condition for my performance?"

"Yes," I said positively. "It should be fine."

The move was not necessarily an ideal choice, since jostling across the thresholds of two rooms and through the doorways might, theoretically at least, affect the tuning. I'd have to check the tuning anyway, I thought to myself. With this much humidity increase, the soundboard is probably rising and the whole mid-section is probably going sharp. Great.

My plan was to get the piano into a place where I could dry it out. I sent the stage manager, who sent an assistant, to find a hair dryer. I checked the tuning. Just a few notes starting to warble.

For the next half hour, while the symphony played Brahms, I blow-dried the piano action. Gently waving the nozzle of the dryer from section to section, I would move the keys with one hand and move the dryer with the other. After about twenty minutes I noticed a definite improvement. The jacks were snapping back sharply. I turned off the hair dryer and touched up the tuning. I figured there would be another twenty minutes before intermission, so after the tuning I turned the dryer to a slightly lower setting and continued the treatment.

The audience was still applauding when the stage crew rushed in for the piano. I turned off the dryer and stood out of their way. The wine had long since peaked, and I dug around in my purse for a piece of gum. Dinner. I picked up my tools and walked to the back of the hall to find a seat. The Beethoven was dazzling, her performance strong and skilled. The piano sounded great. There were two curtain calls.

I can always tell if I'm dealing with a professional performer. The difference really shows up with rock groups. I never have to wait for a stage crew to finish setting up, except when it's a rock group. Then, they have three semi trucks full of gear: Speakers as big as cars, mixing boards the size of corporate board room tables, lights by the hundreds, hanging from the catwalks, poking up around the edges and backdrops. I sit and watch the crew work, often impressively efficient from the experience they have gained, setting up in one town after another just to tear down in the wee hours of morning, load everything back on the trucks, and sleep while the bus driver takes them to the next destination.

If I sit for more than fifteen minutes, I start charging. One time I sat for an hour and a half, tuned for thirty minutes and charged one hundred fifty dollars for my total job. No one ever said a word about it, which made me wonder how much I could have charged.

I had waited about thirty minutes on one rock-and-roll job when the crew chief motioned me onto the stage. I stepped carefully around the thick black cables that crisscrossed behind the band setup, maneuvering between the two huge drum sets and the massive speakers that stood near the little grand piano. It was a nice piano, and I started work immediately. I knew they were pushing for a sound check in thirty minutes, which would cut me too close if I had any major tuning to do.

The piano was not that bad. Tuned for every show, the strings were used to being on pitch. I found myself wondering about the previous tuner, though, when I found many of the basic temperament notes not well positioned. That would mean retuning many of the strings, but it had to be done to suit my judgment.

I worked in fully focused concentration, and I was pleased that I didn't have to struggle to hear over chairs being set up or stage crew conversation. The minutes ticked by, and at one point I turned to a nearby crew member to ask what would happen if I ran a few minutes past four, the time sound check was scheduled.

"It shouldn't be a problem," he said. "We'll do our best to work with you."

"Good," I said. "The tuning was pretty bad, and it's taking me some time to get it right."

So I continued. I had only about another two octaves to clean up unisons when four o'clock came. I figured another five minutes.

What I hadn't figured on was the artist. At precisely four o'clock a young man dressed in a black leather jacket, skin-tight black leather pants, and tall black boots came striding out onto center stage. He reached down for his sparkling red guitar on its chrome stand and fumbled with the strap for a minute. I thought, okay, he'll quietly check his tuning while I finish. I kept on tuning.

After a few more moments of silence, I was suddenly blasted off my seat with an enormous, resonating guitar chord, swiftly followed by another and yet another as the artist strummed his instrument with great flourishes. He tossed his long blonde hair first to one side and then another, as if the hair movement was intimately connected with the motion of his hands on the strings of the guitar.

I sat for a few moments, watching him. At first I thought, okay, this guy for some reason has to hit a few chords, then he'll stop and I can finish. I waited. He continued, the sounds from his cranked-up volume rattling the windows of the huge auditorium and deafening my sensitive hearing. I turned toward a nearby stage hand.

"What is his deal?" I screamed over the din. "I'm not through tuning."

He kind of shrugged. "There's not really anything I can do," he shouted back.

I got the impression that this star was a "case," as my mother would say, and had everybody intimidated. For some reason he believed he should be able to do whatever he wanted to do, and to hell with the rest. I steamed for a few minutes, sitting there with my hearing under assault from the ear-splitting cacophony now pouring from his guitar. I watched his long blonde hair swing from side to side, his body contorting to his inner voices as the music surged from his legs, gut, and head through his shiny red instrument.

I figured I had two choices: pack up and leave or make the s.o.b. be quiet for five minutes. I stood up. I moved toward him from behind the piano and past the computer/synthesizer setup into the open space that was reserved for him, the artist. He caught my movement out of the corner of his eye and tried to ignore me, strumming yet another cluster of chords as his body gestured.

I stood there, about ten feet from him, staring at him, for another minute or two before he stopped and looked at me. The sudden silence was enormous. He didn't say anything, looking at me from his petulant, arrogant pose of power. I refused to be intimidated.

"I can stop tuning now, if you'd like, but the top two octaves are still out of tune," I said slowly, clearly, patiently. I waited for his response.

There was no response, at least nothing verbal. He stared at me as if I were from another planet, then turned abruptly and stomped off the stage, his tight butt twisting in the black leather, his long blonde hair streaming out behind him.

Did he think I was off base with the radical suggestion that his group's piano be in tune? What was his problem? No one came forward to answer my silent questioning as I walked back to the piano. I sat down and finished my work without further interruption. As I was packing up my tool case, a crew hand came up nearby and sheepishly offered an apology.

"Sorry about that," he offered. "There's not really anything we can do when he wants to play. You know."

"Oh," I said sympathetically. "Well, I hope he gets over it soon."

I billed extra for that one. Wear and tear on the ears.

I was booked nearly six months ahead to tune for an annual jazz festival in a nearby resort community. It was a major event, a three-day program which would culminate in a Saturday night concert by an internationally known artist and his group. The artist's advance information made it very clear the piano and piano preparation were major factors. My job would be to arrive early Saturday afternoon and prepare the piano. Following sound check at four, I would return and do a touch-up tuning before the concert and be on hand during the concert to touch up at intermission.

This was quite an undertaking, since the event was over an hour and a half from my home. The event organizers were quite generous, however, and offered to pay a handsome fee, plus give me tickets for the performance, plus provide a suite of rooms (in case I brought guests) for the night. I began to look forward to a little work and a lot of play.

As time progressed toward the event I was contacted by the organizers, specifically by Mr. Jay Edmond, to talk about problems they were having locating a grand that would meet the strenuous requirements of the artist. In booking this artist, they had promised to provide a nine-foot grand, either Steinway or Yamaha, and neither was available in that community. At first, they had assumed the nearest dealer for either brand would be able to rent them an instrument. Unfortunately, the Yamaha dealer had nothing available, and the closest Steinway dealer was one hundred fifty miles away. Finally, it was decided to pay the extra trucking fee to bring a Steinway.

Serious problems arose when, a month before the event, the Steinway dealer informed the organizers that the nine-foot they had planned to rent was not going to be available. In fact, they would have nothing available. Jay called me wanting to know if I could suggest an alternate place to get a grand. He was furious because they had a binding contract with the Steinway dealer. We agreed he should hold them to it.

Which he did. They found a nine-foot in Oklahoma City, requiring transport of over five hundred miles, one way. But they agreed to deliver it for the same price. Everyone was relieved.

The day arrived, a crisp, bright-blue slice of October. I packed up an overnight bag, picked up a friend, and we headed up the curvy, scenic road, marveling at the rich colors of fall. Once my afternoon work was finished, we would have lots of time for a leisurely dinner at one of the many great restaurants around town. Maybe Cajun, I suggested. No, she said, maybe Italian. We decided to wait till we were hungrier to decide.

I let her drop me off and take the car to check us in at the hotel while I worked on the piano. There was a sound crew setting up microphones, a crew I often met at similar events, and we exchanged friendly, sarcastic greetings. I climbed up the steep stage steps and squeezed between the microphones, speakers, and the tail of the piano which were closely fit onto the small stage.

The first thing I noticed was that there was no bench. Not good. We rustled up a chair while somebody's kid went out in search of a proper bench. The second thing I noticed was the thick layer of dirt that covered the piano — the lid, keys, pedals, soundboard, everything, inside and out. I found this alarming. It looked like it had been stored in a barn.

That wasn't the worst, though. I played up and down the keyboard. Several notes continued to hum after I had passed them. Not good. Several notes in the treble were noticeably out of balance with the rest, either too shrill or too soft. Maybe I could voice those. Most disturbing was the drop-off in tonal projection in the bass section. Every single note from the bass break down sounded almost muffled, clearly quieter, weaker, than the tenor and treble. I was afraid that would have no remedy.

At about this point, Jay arrived, anxious to hear my verdict on this piano he had struggled so hard to get. I briefly gave him the report. He was not happy.

"What are we going to do?" he asked, his eyebrows rising ever higher on his forehead. "My God, this guy's rep said the piano had to be *right*! Isn't there anything you can do?"

His light brown hair, so carefully combed upon his arrival, seemed to respond to his agitation, poking up a bit on one side, sliding down in front. He paced the edge of the stage near where I sat on the folding metal chair.

"And what's worse," he went on, his voice rising higher in pitch, "is that I've heard that this guy will walk off a gig if he doesn't like the piano. I mean, he has a *reputation* for doing that!"

"Well, okay," I said, "that does put the pressure on." I thought for a minute. I had two hours before sound check. "We need to get this thing cleaned up. If you can get someone to get some polish and some damp rags I'll go ahead and start tuning. Once I've tuned it, I'll work on voicing the treble. But Jay," I said frankly, "I don't think there is anything we can do about the bass being quiet."

"Oh, God," he said. "Okay, let's do it."

The tuning required a small pitch raise, basically meaning that I would go over the tuning twice. That took an hour and fifteen minutes. Toward the end of that time, Jay returned with a bag full of rags and a new bottle of Pledge. He was going to clean it himself. I sent him out to the men's room to get some of the rags moist, since Pledge was worthless until the dirt layers were gone. After I completed the tunings, I cleaned the strings, soundboard, and plate while Jay continued working on the cabinet. We were making progress.

Back at the keyboard, I pulled out the action mechanism and worked on the high notes, pounding a few hammer tops and needling a few, trying to equalize the tone quality to some middle range. Then I rushed through the dampers, checking to see if there were any adjustments I could make mechanically that would make the faulty dampers work better. But, no, mechanically, it seemed all was working properly. But strings were still sounding after release. So I resorted to drastic measures and pushed the ringing strings closer to the damper, an iffy resolution since the string could move back at any time during the performance and because the hammer would suddenly be striking the string at a new spot. But it worked. One by one the noisy strings were shut up.

At fifteen minutes before the four o'clock sound check, I had done all I thought I could do, except try to improve the bass. Once again I took out the action and tried a fine sanding across the hammers in the bass, then pounded the tips to harden them some. But it was useless. There was a structural problem somewhere, perhaps a poor glue joint between the bridge and the soundboard. Or maybe it had always been this way. Maybe this was why it was stored in a barn.

"I think we should say nothing to the artist," Jay said as I stood up to move off the stage. "After all, he may not notice anything."

"Okay," I agreed. "Let's just keep it quiet and let him rehearse."

Jay and I sat down in the back of the auditorium, across from the main sound man who was still juggling cables going into the mixing board. The sound man and I looked at each other, veterans of this last minute war of nerves to get the machinery to function, the whine out of the microphones, the artists handled. He grinned and I grinned.

"Guess what," he whispered.

I got up and crouched over by where he was working. "What?"

"This guy ordered these special microphones for this job and I don't have them."

"What?!" I whispered back, somewhat alarmed, thinking

of the compromised piano, now the wrong microphones. "What are you going to do?"

"I've got good microphones," he said philosophically. "I'm hooking them up. It's all I can do. Hell," he went on with some emotion, "I called as far as Tulsa and Springfield. No one has those mikes! This isn't the West Coast, for God's sake."

His voice trailed off as he caught some movement in the corner of his eye. "They're here. Damn."

He worked even more furiously with the cables, talking into his headset, asking his crew on stage to test the troublesome microphone center stage as I returned to sit by Jay. The artist and his entourage, including the three other instrumentalists, walked down the dark aisle toward the stage. They were older, in their late fifties. They seemed relaxed, pleased to be enjoying the local cuisine and ambiance on this sparkling autumn day.

Good, I thought to myself. *Maybe they won't be fussy.*

I sat there for the next forty-five minutes, getting up once to go tell my friend who had returned to pick me up that I would have to stay through sound check, so I could be on hand for the artist's input. She agreed to pick me up at six. They played through several pieces, parts here and there of things that sounded vaguely familiar. I am no jazz fan, but it sounded good to me.

The first thing that was a problem was the microphones. I made faces at the sound man as he hiked up and down the aisle, reconnected this and that speaker, a few wires here and there. He rolled his eyes. The sound was not clear on the right side, then the drummer's mikes kept screaming. It took about twenty minutes to get all that worked out. He finally said things were good.

They played some more, getting into their music. The beat slowed for one piece, and I could hear the talent of their work. These guys were good. The piano, though, was clearly unbalanced. There wasn't enough bass. I figured any minute he would have a fit.

But they kept playing, trying starts and stops on what was evidently a new piece. They finished a little early, and Jay rushed down to the stage. He told the artist, the piano player, that I was here, if he needed to talk with me. Which he did. Jay motioned me down.

The artist was a pleasant-looking man, the wiry gray hair escaping in several directions from his partially balding head. He smiled at me with warm brown eyes and shook my hand as I stepped toward the piano. I could see years of traveling, playing unknown spots for one-night stands, his home wherever he could make music happen. I've seen that look before, some kind of trademark on those whose lives are ultimately given, entirely, to the love of music.

"The piano sounds wonderful," he began generously. "The treble is very nice."

He paused and ran a few octaves in the bass. I knew what was coming.

"Is there anything you can do to bring the bass up? It's pretty dead," he said.

I didn't dare glance at Jay, but we both had the same thought. We were holding our breath, expecting the man to leap up from the wiggling, borrowed bench and start screaming about walking out on the show if the piano was not immediately improved or replaced. Instead, this quietly smiling man was willing to ask if we could do anything.

"Well," I sputtered quickly, "I've tried just about everything, to tell you the truth. I've tried to pack the hammers, but it didn't improve. I believe we have some kind of structural problem."

"I am so sorry," Jay said earnestly. "You wouldn't believe what we have been through to get this instrument, and it is just all that is available."

The artist looked at Jay, perhaps bemused at the anxiety in Jay's voice. I wondered if the reputation he had for being a prima donna was a mistake. Or was it for only this time, this event, he had decided to just take it, let it happen? What was going on?

"It'll be fine," he said pleasantly, after a moment.

He turned away from us then, making suggestions to the bassist about moving his stool a little closer to the front of the stage. Jay and I exchanged large-eyed looks and then he followed them as they moved offstage. I could hear the conversation drifting in bits from backstage as I went over the piano's tuning for last-minute adjustments. I wondered about his reaction, so out of character for the reputation that had preceded him.

My friend and I had to settle for a rushed dinner in a not-so-great restaurant that night. We had been so sure we would have plenty of time, we had made no reservations. The town was packed, mostly for the jazz festival, and everyone wanted good food and good wine at a leisurely pace. We only had an hour after I had changed and rested a few minutes.

I sat in the dark theater, my friend next to me, concentrating on the performance. The music was good, for jazz, and I found myself swept along with the mood of the music, complex and inventive in its harmonies and melodies. The saxophone wailed out a plaintive phrase, crying like a heartbroken woman in the night, while the pulse from the bass and the curl of the drumbeat kept up the life rhythms. Behind it, then in the front of the sound, came and went the piano, first with delicate shimmers trailing down the high end and then strongly pushing, tenor and baritone voices singing from the lower notes, mixing in a deep and resonant match to the saxophone's reedy whine.

I knew he was struggling with the piano, his mind forced to pull back from total involvement in the creation of music to concentrate on playing harder in the bass. He would be exhausted by the end of the show, I knew. He worked at the instrument, swaying and driving as the music rushed on and on. Even as he did his best, I could tell in some places where the piano was solo that the bass wasn't giving what was needed. There was no amount of pounding the keys, even if he had wanted to, that could have made the low notes ring richly through the huge crowded room.

The crowd didn't seem to know. They applauded energetically after every piece, whistling and calling him by name at the end, begging for more even after two encores. The show ran an hour longer than expected, and the physical exhaustion was plain to see on each of the performers as they made their last bows, their bodies drenched in sweat.

At some point in the program, after I had made the intermission tuning check, I realized why he had the reputation, why it worked out that show organizers and piano technicians sweat blood before he ever shows up. How many times had he gone to a booking to find a piano in absolutely unplayable condition, keys not working, a half-step below pitch, hammers worn to the core? He'd been in the business thirty years. What better way to make sure of a decent piano than to leak rumors about walking off a show? Helpless as he was to take his instrument with him, at the mercy of whatever town and whoever organized to provide a piano that would be his creative medium, he had at least the power of an outrageous reputation.

In fact, he just wanted to make music. The reputation would get him the best instrument he could get. Then it was left to the musician in him to sit at it, play it, work at it, bend it to his will, make it speak his voice, even if it had been stored in a barn. This guy was a pro.

10

Old Folks' Homes

"My piano is my best friend," Mrs. Mansing said to me, shortly after I arrived at her tiny apartment. I was busy opening the top, taking the front panel off, and preparing to tune. There was almost no room to move around the piano. An ancient dressing table with matching mirror and stool sat next to the piano, its darkened maple surface laden with a small lamp, two miniature pianos set on crocheted table scarves, a green vase, several colorful little statuettes of rosy-cheeked children doing interesting things: fishing, walking with school books, picking flowers.

"Once I thought I would sell my piano," Mrs. Mansing continued. "I woke up in the middle of the night and thought about not having it, and I was alarmed that I would have thought of selling it."

"So you really enjoy playing it?" I inquired, to respond encouragingly to her conversation.

"Oh, yes," she said warmly, her eyes lighting up as she looked toward the piano. I noticed how her small, bent body seemed to lean slightly to the right and wondered if she had suffered a stroke. Perhaps that was why her family had her here in this "residential retirement complex," as the sign outside had so euphemistically stated.

"Yes," she said. "I play a lot, not that I play very well." She showed me her gnarled hands, the skin thin enough to show the bluish veins where they passed over the bones and tendons in little humps and curves, rising and falling like a road moving through valleys and hills in a rural country-side. The translucent skin crinkled like old parchment as it clumped around her knuckles, and I wondered how many dishes she had washed, how many times she had smoothed her now-white hair back from the sides of her face.

"Oh," I said heartily, "I'm sure that it is wonderful to sit and play. I know it gives me a good break from everything to just sit and play the piano."

She nodded in agreement, and busied herself moving papers around on the small table that stood directly behind me as I faced the piano. The table was covered with stacks and boxes of papers, some of which were so close to the piano bench where I was sitting that I could have read the words if I had wanted. In fact, I saw that there were letters in at least two of the boxes, typed on onion skin paper and creased from being folded and mailed. I was careful not to read any of it.

She apologized for the cramped space, explaining that she had not yet had time to sort through all the things that needed sorting since she had moved. I got the idea that she had lived alone for several years, perhaps since the death of her husband, and the accumulated records of a family's life-time, now boxed and moved to a much more compact resi-dence, would have to be severely culled, a job she might despise or relish, or both.

The piano was considerably off pitch, but I decided to

not put myself, the woman, or the piano through a pitch raise. It had obviously been tuned at this lower pitch level for years, since even the highest and lowest notes were correspondingly low. I knew strings might break if I pushed it up to concert pitch, and what would be gained? I wondered to myself. Mrs. Mansing would never play with other instruments, and neither would she know by ear that her A was a half-note lower than the universal A-440. Besides, it would cost extra for the pitch raise, and the tuning would require follow-up to get the thing stabilized, and it seemed apparent she didn't have lots of money.

I told her what I had in mind, and she agreed it would be best to leave it, at least for now. Later, she said, after she had caught up from the move, perhaps next year, she might be interested in getting it put on pitch. I set to work on the tuning, and she busied herself in the adjoining bedroom, probably putting away clothes I thought, since I could hear drawers opening and closing, and occasionally the clash of coat hangers scraping along the bar in the closet.

I wondered what kind of house Mrs. Mansing had left behind. She moved back and forth in her little rooms as I worked through my tuning. At one point she asked if I'd like a cup of coffee, which I refused, and it seemed that she had been adept at the social graces in her life, comfortable at bridge club or church luncheons. I wondered how many years she had struggled with the inexorable bowing of her back as the calcium slowly drained out of her bones, wondered how she came to accept the aging of a female form that had once been young and alluring, fertile and strong.

Her small apartment, located at the end of the hall of this dormitory-style building, contained a tiny kitchen, living room, bath, and bedroom. The whole space was probably not more than eighteen by twenty-four feet, and it reminded me of all the other retirement home spaces where I had been to tune other pianos, instruments of varying quality saved through decades of children growing up, family crises, indebtedness, moves, and now this, saved because it embodied strong memories or offered respite from the turmoil, a few quiet notes strung together with the harmonies of major and minor chords.

There had been one woman who had moved into her tiny space with a six-foot grand, its ornate walnut cabinet resting proudly in the whole of her allotted living room with only one armchair and small bookcase wedged along a wall beside it. She had told me she'd rather not have her couch or her other living room furniture if it meant giving up her piano. Her volumes of Beethoven sonatas, Bach, and Chopin were stacked on the bookcase shelves, the pages yellowing and shattering along the often-turned edges.

In another woman's retirement apartment, a brand new upright, shiny and black, stood along one wall of her immaculate, miniature living room, a gift from her children for giving up the rambling family home to live in a compromised but secure place for her remaining years. She hadn't quite made friends with the piano yet. It seemed set apart from the coziness of her over-stuffed, pale green couch and armchair with Queen Anne legs. She was pleased with the generous gift, I could tell, but I could also see her hesitant emotion over a move made to please concerned children but not quite pleasing to her.

My mind wandered as my hands moved methodically across the keyboard, tuning one string and then the next as

Mrs. Mansing rummaged in her bedroom. I remembered my own grandmother, my dearest relative as a child, who would hug me up against her thick, soft body with a quick pat and a chuckle, who patiently showed me how to hold the crochet hook in one hand, how to loop the coarse white thread through the fingers of the other hand, and like magic, little loops, strings, and finally intricate designs emerged from the clumsy workings of my two young hands.

Grandma didn't have any money, but her Christmas presents were prized, like the doll she had made out of unbleached muslin, its head, body, and limbs stuffed out rounded with cotton before she had stitched them together with rough, thick thread. She had painted on its features, wide-open blue eyes with tiny lashes, a rosebud mouth that tilted upwards at the corners in some secret amusement. The dress was a pale purple print, a flour-sack piece that could have been twenty years old by the time it was used for my doll. It smelled like her, somehow unaffected by the sulfur in the tap water or the grease from her frying pans, fresh and sharp like newly turned dirt in her garden.

The doll was soft, and its stitch-jointed limbs moved realistically as I acted it through make-believe scenes of life. There was no hard plastic to feel cold against me if I hugged it, and no Barbie breasts jutting out to define an ideal woman's body that I might later compare myself to. Just last Christmas — and maybe too late with them now nearly twenty — I gave my daughters cloth dolls I found at a craft shop, made by the same pattern as my grandmother's, soft and white and adorned with angel wings, made in China.

When Grandma was eighty, she was still able to tell me her recipe for lye soap, scrawled on a small piece of white paper somewhere in my recipe file. I tried it once, starting with rendering fresh lard and working over a huge, black iron pot with a wood fire built under it in my backyard. I overcooked the pig scraps, which gave a sooty cast to the lard. And somehow I did something wrong, maybe when I mixed in the can of lye, because the soap was grainy when it finally cooled in the wax-paper-lined pans. I was proud anyway. It wasn't great soap, but it was soap.

But by the time Grandma was eighty-six she couldn't take care of herself. My dad and his sister were both constantly upset because Grandma would get lost in a neighbor's backyard and not be able to find her way home, or because she would think it was November and bring all her pots of flowers inside when in fact it was clearly June. She gave up cooking and every day had toast and jelly. They paid a woman to stay with her for a long time, but then bits and pieces of things caused them to think the woman was abusing Grandma, and so they finally decided to put her in a "home."

It was the nicest place they could afford. They tried to visit often. Grandma hated the whole idea, frequently complaining that the attendants stole her things, that she didn't know any of those people, that she wanted to go back home. When I saw her, she begged me to take her home. She looked bedraggled and gaunt. She missed her cats; she needed to hoe in her garden. I was distraught with the situation.

She had only been there two or three months when she fell and broke her hip. She had escaped, not for the first time, this time inching her way across an icy parking lot to hide in a car. When the attendants found her, she fought with them. Somehow in the struggle, she fell on the icy concrete. She ended up in the hospital with a broken hip.

It was a hospital for geriatric cases, so after they set her hip, they moved her into a room there. She wasn't supposed to move, but within a day or two she wanted to get up. The catheter bothered her, so she pulled it out, determined to take herself to the bathroom if she needed to. She fought off attendants and nurses, angered that they wanted to keep needles fastened in her arm. Finally, they sedated her and strapped her down.

Grandma on Thorazine was more than I could take. I couldn't go see her. When a week had gone by, and my dad told me she was refusing food and water, I silently cheered her on. I sent her mental messages, how much I loved her, how I hoped she could be released from her torment. She died just a few days later, and I was thankful.

I thought of the other old people I have seen, many less fortunate than Mrs. Mansing and relegated to single rooms in nursing homes, their decline in some way similar to that of my grandma. Those homes smell strongly of antiseptic, with an almost perceptible underlying scent of urine and sweat, and somehow, the residual odor of sauerkraut and wieners. The pianos of these establishments, located in the dining room or the front lobby, are invariably miserable little instruments incapable of producing music of even average quality, serviced about once every ten years as the generous gift of some concerned relative.

In one such home, I went to a piano that sat along the inside wall of the front lobby, a large spacious room with big windows on the three sides that surrounded the entry door. In the middle of the fourth, interior wall was the hallway that went to the heart of the building, its sides lined with the doors of the many rooms. Several groups of chairs and couches were spread around the front room, and a large television sat in the corner on the other side of the hallway entrance from the piano.

One of my first hurdles had been to simply get the television turned down, with a few muttered complaints from the seven or eight who were watching it. A second hurdle was to try to hear well enough to tune over the constant hum, the institutional hum that I notice in cafeterias, restaurants, meeting rooms. Some combination of ice machine, central heating furnaces, large appliances, a hundred people breathing. It wasn't a loud hum, and with a decent piano it wouldn't have made such a difference. But the hammers were worn away, and every hit of the key produced so much wobbling, clicking, scraping, and thumping that the production of a tone from the string was a kind of afterthought.

A third obstacle I soon had to overcome was a man who came into the room a short time after I actually started tuning. He moved slowly, carefully placing the aluminum walker in front of him with each dragging step, his aged black slacks cinched in tight around his thin waist with a narrow black belt. His white dress shirt was limp, and the sleeves were sloppily rolled up to his elbows. I tried not to notice him, as I tried not to look at any of those who continued to sit in the corner, staring at the now-silent television, or the others who sat scattered around the room. Noticing might mean eye contact, which was an unspoken invitation for them to come over to me and talk.

Soon after moving his walker toward a chair and seating himself, this man began to complain in a loud, reedy voice.

"What's she doing over there?!" he exclaimed first. No one paid any attention. I glanced his way. He was looking down at his hands spread out in front of him on a small, empty card table. I continued tuning.

"That's a terrible racket she's making over there!" he announced irritably. Patiently, others nearby explained that "she" was tuning the piano. "What?" he inquired. They repeated the information. He got quiet for a while, absently stroking his thinning black hair from its low part across the top of his balding head. Then, "Is she supposed to be playing that thing?" And he began to sing loudly, unmusically, using "lo, lo" and "la, la" for syllables as if by making his own noise he could block out mine. Shaking my head to myself slightly, I continued to tune. Working around his outbursts was about the only thing I could do.

He was in a muttering stage when the door alarm went off, and I looked around to see a plump, short woman walking slowly from the exit toward the side yard. She was looking up toward the sky, then around herself, and seemed to be forcing her body to move faster, walk further. Her sparse white hair was flying around her head like swirls of cotton candy, and her tight, faded pink slacks dragged at the heels where they came down over the tops of her fuzzy house shoes. The alarm kept ringing, and a few others went to stand by the windows and door, silently watching her scuffling down the sidewalk toward the street in agitated slow motion. Finally, two male attendants came from the hallway and shut off the alarm. They went out the door and walked steadily toward the escaping woman. One stood on either side of her, and they seemed to be trying to reason with her. Then, moving her along between them, they turned back toward the door. I thought I could feel her despair, but maybe she just didn't know where she was.

For the time of her escape, though, I tuned without interruption from the man, his anger at my disruption momentarily forgotten as he watched what seemed like a routine drama in their daily life. After the attendants had brought the woman back in and re-armed the alarm things settled back down, and soon he was yelling again. The woman escapee stood by a window, staring out toward the west, perhaps toward a destination in her fantasy of autonomy.

"Somebody needs to tell that woman over there she can't play worth a damn!" the man piped up. And then he again sang loudly. "La la la, hm hm, lo lo, lo lo."

After I had finished doing the best I could do on the piano, I packed up my tools. I announced to those still huddled around the silent television that I was finished, and immediately they turned up the volume for the last few minutes of *The Price Is Right*.

I thought I might make eye contact with the man on my way toward the front door. The chair where he was sitting was only a few feet from the main walkway toward the entrance. I walked slowly past him, looking toward him for the opportunity to give him at least a reassuring smile, perhaps a comment that okay, now I was done. But even as I paused nearby, he never looked up. Instead, he concentrated on his hands, long and thin and pale, stretched out flat against the worn brown Naugahyde table top, seemingly oblivious to me, the room, the world. I didn't understand.

I was nearing the end of Mrs. Mansing's piano tuning. I noted that her living room not only held the piano, the vanity, and the small table behind me that was piled with the boxes of papers, but also an easy chair, a couch, two end tables, coffee table, desk with a television sitting on it, a large china cabinet, and assorted floor lamps, chairs, boxes, and unhung paintings. There was barely room to maneuver from one place to the next. I wondered how she got around. Taking the last of my tools off the cabinet, I began putting the piano back together. Mrs. Mansing appeared in the room.

"How is my piano?" she asked. "I bought that in 1939, and it's been pretty good."

"It's in good shape," I told her, recognizing by her tone that she wanted reassurance that the piano was not deteriorating. Of course, by concert standards, that wouldn't have been true, but we weren't on a stage somewhere. We were in Mrs. Mansing's new living room in her tiny apartment in one of three dormitory buildings that all connected at the cafeteria building on a cul-de-sac that circled in front of the "residential retirement complex." "The piano is doing great. But it will need another tuning in about a year."

She tore her check off with a flourish and handed it to me with slightly unsteady hands. "Okay," she said. "I'll call in a year. Maybe we can do something about that pitch then. What do you think?"

I considered it for a moment. "I think that would be fine, if that's what you want to do. We can sure get it fixed up if you want."

"Yes," she said. "I think I'd like that. I'll call. We'll work on it next year."

Women in the Woods

Maudine Breedlove lived — and I say "lived" instead of "lives" because I haven't heard from her in six years — on the edge of a town called St. Joe that passed its prime sometime before 1930. The railroad used to go out there when the town was bustling with citizens and industry, which was mostly the logging of the nearby virgin hardwood forest. Huge trees fell to the loggers' saws. Then, trimmed of their thick branches, they were loaded onto sturdy wagons pulled by teams of mules, stacked up on flat railroad cars that the steam engines would carry back to the main lines and, from there, transported to local towns and big cities back east. There they became long, six-by-twelve-inch floor beams and overlap siding, or sturdy oak rocking chairs, fine cherry bed sets, and walnut armoires.

The road into St. Joe winds through the long valley and begins to climb into the reforested hills, past the old schoolhouse that still sits up on the hillside overlooking the town, its high roof sagging where the weight of snow and ice and the summer heat on the shingles has pressed down on the long oak rafters and roof joists. Adorning the faded red roof is the bell tower, a little square cap of peeling white paint with its own tiny roof and sides louvered so the peals of the school bell could escape to echo across the narrow valley. The local folks have tried to keep the school building from complete decay, working with love and no money, but since the fifties, when the schools were consolidated, the building is only occasionally used for town meetings or a craft show.

When I came to tune Maudine Breedlove's piano, I knew I'd not find a place to eat lunch. There was no grocery store, no restaurants. A barber shop sat along the main street near the tiny, one-room post office, and beyond that an old hardware store building hosted the newest business in town, a video rental. Antiques shops occupied the long-closed mercantile building and the adjoining rock structure that probably used to be a drug store, the faded Coca-Cola advertisement still legible on its west side.

There was an auto garage near the end of the street, where the dirt driveway and gravel lot at the side of the square, sheet-metal building were stained black with decades of lost oil and rear-end grease, where old tires and rusting wheel rims were piled up along the outside of the north wall with odd-shaped pieces of metal and fifty-five-gallon drums. The metal roof was splotched with rust, and a steel stove pipe ran up a few feet into the air from it, a cascade of burned-brown creosote stain painting its sides and streaking down the roof beneath. In the warm months, the big garage door stood open and the casual passerby might see a man in his dirty white T-shirt and jeans bending as he worked underneath an aging Ford or Chevy pickup truck, his muscled arms wielding some long wrench against the front axle where it engaged the wheel, his red shop rag hanging from a rear pocket. Other men might stand nearby, their bodies cast into resting positions by throwing a hip out sideways to balance their weight on one side, or by leaning against the doorway and propping one foot back against the wood, their jaws packed with a fresh chew of tobacco, their comments laconic and occasional.

When the folks got hungry, they went home to eat. The closest restaurant was twenty-five miles back toward the bigger cities, and about half the year even that one was closed, since it catered more to the tourists who travel in warmer weather down to the national park where they can swim or climb the bluffs. After that, you have to go another twenty miles to get to a place that would reliably serve burgers or chicken-fried steak with mashed potatoes, salad, two vegetables, rolls, and iced tea for $3.95, summer or winter.

I passed through the town slowly on my way to Maudine's house. For about a ten-mile stretch before St. Joe, the highway follows the mounded remains of the old railroad bed where it traveled to its logging stops. I envisioned the old days when horses stood in wait at storefronts, when women in long dresses ordered a piece of cloth or a sack of flour at the general store, when men in leather boots strode down the wooden sidewalks to meet and talk at the blacksmith's shop. The land remembers them, not just in the straight green mound of the old rail bed, but in acres of land with no old-growth trees and decaying remains of abandoned homesteads where the only thing still standing is a part of the stone chimney or the rock fence that once ran alongside the house, where jonquils and overgrown forsythia bloom yellow every spring.

As my car wound up the hill along the high riverbank and the town slipped behind me, I could almost see the ghosts of the early days in the rushes of my peripheral vision, the barefoot children running down a grassy path along the hillside toward the proud new schoolhouse. My mother actually lived here once as a child, when her family followed the logging boom to find an income during the Depression. She went to school in that house, barefoot like the rest.

A mile and a half beyond the edge of St. Joe, I turned right down a narrow dirt road that follows the side of the river for a while before it winds up another steep hill, away from the confined, green valley. About halfway up the rocky hill road, I saw her name, as promised, on the mailbox and turned the car in a sharp left to get into her driveway. The house sat just below the short drive, positioned on the south-facing hill terrace to stare off across the valley to the hills beyond, blue and then faded blue in the distance.

Her rusting wire fence ran from the back edges of the house around the backyard, held in place by aging metal fence posts. The old wrought-iron gate shrieked on its little hinges as it turned open. The backyard was mostly paved with wide, flat, brown stones, pulled from nearby higher ground where the flagstone cropped out in straight layers like crackers in a package. A tiny garden plot sat off to the right, thick with deep green tomato plants and a few paler green yellow squash plants, a couple of short rows of potatoes whose vines were thick with dark and purple-veined leaves. In borders around the edges of the yard, running along the wire fence, were beds of multicolored four-o'clocks, red geraniums, and yellow marigolds. Petunias bloomed in the old original shades of purple; hollyhocks in pink and burgundy stood tall near the back door. I just wanted to sit there, to rest and breathe in the warm fragrant air of this woman's wonderful garden.

I knocked loudly at the sagging screen door, warned by her on the phone that she couldn't hear very well. There was no response. I yelled out her name as I knocked for the second time. I could see inside the back porch through the screen, where her black rubber boots leaned against a stack of bulging cardboard boxes and rows of clean glass canning jars lined up along the house wall. An old wooden table sagged under the weight of stacked old magazines and hand tools and flower pots, piled up with cotton garden gloves, rags, a few old pans, a box of rock salt. In the corner near the house door stood a group of yard tools: a rake, shovel, leaf rake and four-pronged hoe, another regular hoe with its blade shortened nearly by half from years of assault against the rocky soil and repeated dressings with a metal file.

The door soon opened, and this woman named Maudine came out across the wooden porch floor toward me, her white hair wrapped up in a flowered scarf whose bright pink and yellow colors picked up the flush in her rosy cheeks. With twinkling eyes and a smile on her face, she told me how glad she was to see me, opening the screen door out toward me. Her soft wrinkled skin smelled like powder as I walked past her with my tools, my tall frame dwarfing her tiny one in the passing.

We walked through her kitchen, spotless but redolent with past cookings of grape jelly, biscuits, chicken with sage. A small yellow-and-white speckled Formica dinette table hosted her salt and pepper shakers, a milk glass vase with a handful of honeysuckle, and some prescription bottles all sitting in a clump on a faded plastic doily. All but one of the four chairs were full of things like newspapers, a Wal-Mart sack stuffed with something, a jacket hanging on the back. On the clean but faded vinyl cabinet tops her canisters of flour, sugar, cornmeal, and oats lined up against the wall, a line continued by jars of twist-ties, cash register receipts, rubber bands, hard candies, clothespins. Her white enamel teapot sat on the stove, and she turned toward it, asking me if I'd have a cup of tea, which I accepted in an odd departure from my norm.

The piano was in the living room, just a few steps beyond the kitchen on the other side of the wall behind the stove. Its tall cabinet had turned dark with age as the varnish had thickened from light and oxidation, but no chips or loose veneer marred the overall appearance. It stood underneath a hanging row of framed family photographs, some slightly off kilter as though in their distance up the wall from Maudine's short body they taunted her with rambunctious misbehavior. Maudine and her husband, newly wed, posed faded in sepia tones with their young, gangly bodies dressed in wedding finery. Maudine and two other women, probably sisters, positioned in sideways turns, smiled toward the camera. Five children stood in front of a small frame house, two boys dressed in overalls and white shirts with their unruly hair creeping up in little thrusts from recent slicking down, three girls in print dresses, the youngest with long pigtails hanging on either side of her neck, the oldest standing back from the others with her hands clasped in front of her skirt, her hair pulled tight, her face aware of poverty as the others were not.

Tuners had been to the piano before and challenged its obstinate plan to stay wildly out of tune. This day it remembered some of its training and responded to my ministrations. Maudine brought me a cup of tea, and I briefly sat with her on the over-stuffed navy blue couch, noting the small figurines of deer and rabbit on her mahogany coffee table, the glass birds, the white crocheted lace borders on the table scarf. We talked about the warm weather, the trouble she had been having with her arthritis in her hands, how it kept her from playing the piano as much as she would have liked. She told me that one of her sons and his family recently came down from Kansas City to visit on Memorial Day, that they had gone down to the cemetery where her husband was buried to decorate the grave with a new lilac bush, since the first one she'd planted years ago had died.

She sighed over being dependent on a few remaining dear and faithful neighbors who would pick her up and take her shopping, since she never learned to drive, and I heard her unspoken wistfulness at the loss of her vitality, her increasing vulnerability to cold winters, deep-rooted weeds in the tomatoes, and loose boards on the house siding. I felt a kinship to her for some reason, perhaps that she reminded me of my grandmother, or that I imagined myself aging like her, living alone someday and focusing my dwindling energy on a tiny perfect garden, sitting in my own living room staring out across the Ozark hills and valleys from my timeworn couch.

As I sipped tea from her delicate china cup, I was torn between my desire to finish work and hurry off to the rest of my appointments and my sudden need to sit with her. I seemed to lapse into a meditative state, her companionship undemanding and somehow reassuring. She said little, willing and happy to sit with me as we gazed through her living room window. The insects droned outside, and the warm, sweet-smelling air filled my nose and my mind with a magic potion of timelessness.

My mind wandered to other women whose homes also felt comfortable to me when I came to service their pianos. There was one woman who lived further out in the woods than Maudine, her small bungalow built in a thick stand of oak on a hillside that sloped gently away behind the house. I can't remember her name. She proudly showed me the violin she had played in the Little Rock symphony in her younger days, kept now in a worn black case on top of her old upright piano. She told me about her noted career in journalism before she had retired, somewhat wistful over the pace and push of getting a newspaper written and into print every day. Her hands, worse than Maudine's, had been crippled with arthritis for long enough that her fingers slanted together in a painful tension between the stiff enlarged knuckles and the tendons that longed for release. It enraged her, I could see, that her time of promise in old age and its ripe pleasure had been handicapped. She explained that she hired a neighbor to do things she couldn't, stubbornly refusing to give up her thoughtful solitude. She could still peck out a few tunes on the piano, but no more two-handed forays into the dark depths of Beethoven.

And another woman living alone, Gladys Hindeman, sprang to my mind as I sat there on Maudine's restful blue couch. Gladys was almost elfin, so tiny and bright-eyed, a constant challenging amusement lurking at the corners of her mouth. I found her quite skilled at the piano, seated at her seven-foot Baldwin grand like a craftsman at his bench and masterfully able to produce waves of music that swept through her small house like a rising storm and broke to the outside to rush past the trees and vines and down toward the waters of the lake.

Her property was not as remote as Maudine's, just a mile

down a rough dirt lane from the main road, readily accessible to the several who came or brought children to take lessons from her. Her cottage was perched on a partially cleared hillside, and from the windows of her sun porch I could easily see through the bare trees to the expanse of the lower Beaver Lake, a man-made wonder filling miles of winding valleys behind the enormous dam.

In the dull light of the overcast day when I last visited Gladys I watched the waters sparkle across the wide inlet that ran from the bottom edge of Gladys's piece of land out toward the far shore's cliffs. No boats marred the scene, painted in slashes and jabs of gray, dark gray, brown, dark brown, light gray. Stiff winds were roughing up the water's surface, making diminutive waves whose peaks picked up the glare of the bright gray sky. I stood away from her as she checked my tuning, running scales from top to bottom, playing a bit of a Chopin mazurka.

She had been losing ground, I had noticed, over the five-year term that I called on her. She had become forgetful and frail. She told me her children had pleaded, urged, and finally prevailed in moving her to Montana, where she would live with her daughter and her family. She was afraid they would sell her piano, but she also knew they had no place to put it. Her voice trailed off as she told me.

As she continued to play, the wind tossed the treetops outside like a conductor with multiple brown batons. She had managed alone here for over twenty years. What would happen to her precious collection of music and primitive musical instruments? I wondered. I thought of how far she had come from her poor beginnings. She had once shown me a photograph of her family when she was just a girl, the parents and children standing in front of their sod house where it nestled in a faint curve of the land in the great expanse of western Kansas. She had proudly described her years at the music conservatory, listed names of great musicians she had studied with, revealed a cultured life of teaching. How could she bear the loss of her piano?

Abruptly, it seemed I had sat on Maudine's couch too long. The tea left in the bottom of my cup was cold, and I set it down on the coffee table as I stood up. Maudine stood up, too, and carried the cups into her kitchen. I methodically finished the tuning. I took out a small rag and cleaned off her keys, dusted a few inner parts, and then put the massive cabinet back together. Sitting on the swaying bench, I let my hands drift across the keys in some hymns from her old church books, playing favorites of mine like "Abide with Me" and "It Is Well with My Soul." The piano faithfully responded, singing into the small house with clear, sweet tones.

Call me in a year or two, I told Maudine as she walked me out to the car, even though I knew that she might not ever call. She did call a few times over the next four or five years, but then nothing. I wouldn't know if she failed to call because the piano still sounded good to her, or because her arthritis got too bad, or because her meager pension got too thin, or because she had joined her husband under the new lilac.

The gate shrieked at me again as Maudine opened it for me, her soft voice and cheery smile thanking me for coming and taking care of her piano. It was one of the first things her husband ever bought for her, she told me as I loaded my tool case into the car. It's been a good piano all these years, she said, and I agreed that it had held up well, that she should get plenty more years of good service from it.

And then I got in the car, started the engine, and drove away, like I did at Gladys's house and the countless other houses I have left with the women who live in these hills with their pianos. Maudine waved at me from the gate, her frail body framed in a profusion of colorful blossoms and greenery, her little white house perched on the rocky hillside in a brief clearing of the thick woods.

12

Churches

Most churches use pianos, even when they have other kinds of instrumental music. Therefore, people who work on pianos get used to going to service church pianos. There is a certain attitude I feel is required for church piano service, a respectful demeanor, a slightly lower voice than usual when walking around in the building — at least in the sanctuary — and perhaps a willingness to give a ten or fifteen percent discount off the regular tuning price in consideration of the fact that the work is more or less for the Almighty, or at least that's how the people who work at the church see it.

I learned these pointers from my dad, who tuned pianos for so many different churches he lost count thirty years ago. Some of this business volume comes from churches who will call for a tuning once every ten years, and by then they have forgotten who they used before, or the person doing the calling isn't the same person as before, so they may never have the same tuner come twice. With an ad in the yellow pages, we get lots of one-time calls like that.

A call came once from a little church over in the west part

of the county, about an hour out of town, almost all highway time. Just a short distance down a dirt lane, the white building sat up along a gentle slope above a rocky creek bottom, and the land around it was cleared and kept mowed. In that summer month, the grass was thick and deep green, and the nearby trees and underbrush were thick with vines and luxurious rambling growth.

It was a concrete block building, about twenty-four by forty feet, with about ten rows of pews on each side of the central aisle and a small raised area in front of a baptistery, up one step from the rest of the floor. On this small platform was the wooden pulpit and about eight chairs behind it, where I guessed other instrumentalists sat. There were amplifiers and tambourines and boxes of tissues. I supposed the tissues were so that when the spirit came over the worshippers, and the tears of joy or repentance flowed, no one would have to go looking for them.

The piano sat to the north end of the little stage, a surprisingly modern, short-style spinet in what appeared to be good condition. As I opened the top lid, the man who had let me in said they didn't know for sure if it really needed tuning, but the real problem was that a lot of the keys didn't work last week for services. This week they had worked a little better, but still lots of keys didn't play like they were supposed to, or so the piano player had said.

I took off the music desk, concerned about a possible humidity problem here in this concrete block church built so close to the creek. The keys were fairly clean, a few mouse droppings here and there but no big nests. I pointed out to him that mice would destroy the piano if left to themselves and recommended setting some poison bait or traps inside the bottom part. But the keys themselves were not sticking, which would have been the clearest clue to high humidity.

Starting to play key by key, I felt some resistance in a large section of the keyboard, as though something was blocking the strike of the hammer. I peered down into the mechanism but I didn't see anything. Usually, a pencil or ruler or piece of music will work its way down into the dropped-action pianos and cause this kind of resistance. I got out my flashlight and started looking carefully, probing with my long tweezers.

Soon I brought up a piece of what at first I thought was thin white cloth. Then I thought it was some kind of tissue paper. I reached down again for another piece of whatever it was, since it was stuffed around in the mechanism for quite a length. With a second larger piece now to examine, I realized what I was looking at. It was a snake's skin.

And it had been a large one. I opened the lower kick-board, moving slowly because I wasn't sure if the snake had left yet, and then got the panel out of my way. Squatting there I could see where the snake had entered the mechanism on the high end and woven itself around the hammer shanks and abstracts and action struts for almost the entire length of the action before dropping down to scrape off the rest of its skin around the pedal trapwork. In places, the shape of its body was still completely preserved, and I could see that the snake's body must have been as big around as my forearm. From the total expanse of the skin I picked out of that piano, I'd say it was at least seven feet long, probably an old black snake, harmless unless you've got eggs, baby chickens, or mice you don't want eaten.

It took me about fifteen minutes to clean out all the skin. The man was accommodating, finding a grocery bag which he held for me to put the skin in. Then I tuned the piano, a service it truly did need. I charged fifteen dollars extra for the snake skin removal. I didn't tell the man that the reason the keys hadn't played at all for their services last week was probably that the snake was in there right then. He might have figured it out, but I hope he didn't tell the lady who had sat there playing that day with her knees just inches away from a seven-foot snake.

I was driving in heavy traffic that was moving fast on a hot afternoon in September on my way to a church tuning. I had passed several slower vehicles and would have preferred to stay in the passing lane, but a large car was looming in my rearview mirror. I try to work with other drivers, so I maneuvered into the right lane so he could go by.

I noted that it was a late model Cadillac, gleaming softly in pale yellow and chrome. It was clean, and I was somewhat amused that as I observed the interior, the upholstery was the same gentle yellow and seemed to surround the heavy-set male driver like a marshmallow. I dismissed him as just another rich person.

However, as the car sped past me I was shocked to discover a sedate yet forthright sign in the rear window, black block letters on a gold, approximately three-by-twelve-inch background stating "Pastor," followed by a cross. As it turned out, he arrived at the same church that was my destination. Tuning the mediocre piano in the comfort of the luxurious chapel, I found it difficult to comprehend how this person, Mr. Pastor, could provide spiritual comfort to his congregation, much less teach the inspired word of the Lord, while finding it necessary as he did to haul his corpulent flesh around in a late-model, pale yellow Cadillac.

I had serviced one church several times over a period of about six years and then had not heard from them for another three or four. I assumed they had found another tuner, which, as I have mentioned, is not an uncommon event for churches. It was a well-established church, built in trimmed limestone blocks before the turn of the century. The ancient wooden pews were ornately carved on each end, and the old oak floors creaked when people moved up and down the aisles.

The equally ancient upright piano stood over to the side in a little alcove, where dark red velvet curtains on either side boldly contrasted the dark wood paneling. A brass plate was mounted on the front, stating in a flourish that it had been the generous gift of Mrs. Edith Irene Sherer, October 17, 1921.

I had tuned it each time I visited with increasing concern that this congregation would soon need to buy a new piano. The action mechanism was worn out, hammers flopped sideways on their way to the strings, and many bridle straps were broken. Worse, the tuning pins were so loose that I often had to tap pins in deeper just to get each tuning to hold, and many of the pins were tapped in as deep as they would go.

Once when I was there tuning, the pastor was available, so I decided to have "the talk." Not that "the talk" about a piano is as serious as "the talk" when it's a terminal illness of a loved one, but it is serious. Especially when it has an engraved brass plate.

I showed him the problems, explaining as I went along that although repairs could be done, they would have to involve complete rebuilding and, therefore, would be quite expensive. In fact, the cost to properly repair the piano would have been more than the purchase price of a new piano. And that would have been a new piano of good quality, such as a studio or upright size.

After hearing his concerns about budget limits, I urged him to look at several options, including replacement with a newer used piano. That way, I explained, they would have a useful instrument for many more years without having the expense of a brand new one. We agreed that it was sad to write off an old workhorse like this piano had been, but I saw that he understood just how senseless it would be to try to patch it up with any kind of half-way repairs.

After this conversation I was not called back for three or four years. I wondered a few times if I had offended him somehow when talking about the piano. Then one day I got a call. A new pastor, rotated in as is the practice of this denomination, said their piano needed tuning and asked if I could come for an appointment.

On the agreed date, I entered the church office to greet the pastor. He was a friendly man and took pleasure in telling me as we walked to the sanctuary how happy they had been that a church patron had contributed the money, a generous amount of five hundred dollars, to restore the piano. *Restore?* I became a bit uneasy. Not for five hundred dollars.

We entered the sanctuary, where the afternoon light glowed through the old stained-glass windows and cast strangely colored radiance across the dark wooden pews. I saw the piano almost immediately, its familiar brass plate gleaming in the orange light. The pastor was telling me about the work that had been done, how all the insides were new now and how glad they were to have been able to keep the instrument. But, he said, it needed tuning.

My first thought was that maybe a retired piano technician had done the needed work for a token fee. There was no other explanation that came readily to mind. I asked him how recently the work had been done. Oh, he said, just within the last few weeks. I asked why the person doing the work hadn't tuned it. He said he didn't know, that the man who did it was retired and only did certain things. He didn't tune. Tuning is the easy part, I thought to myself. Why wouldn't he tune it?

I opened the top lid and took off the front panel. The entire mechanism stood before me in all its glory, every last bit of it just the exact same as it had been the last time I came to tune. No hammers had been replaced, or even reshaped, or even cleaned. The original dirt that coated the whole thing was still intact. I hurriedly glanced at the bridle straps. Same bridles, except now there were more broken.

I wondered briefly if I was in the twilight zone. I took my flashlight out of my tuning case and examined the tuning pins closely. Exactly the same as before, same rust, same dirt, same strings, same coils, many of which were driven right up to the gilding on the cast-iron plate. I turned to the pastor.

"Just what exactly did this person restore?" I asked. As far as I could tell, absolutely nothing had been done.

"Everything," the pastor said, in a troubled tone of voice. "He said all new felts, new strings, new everything."

I pointed to things. "These are the hammers, and they are the original ones. And these tuning pins." I looked at him. "Nothing has been done."

"But we paid him five hundred dollars," he said. "And I saw him take this thing out," pointing to the action. I could tell he was getting upset.

I was shaking my head. How could somebody be so incredibly bold, I thought, to come in, lie, lie, lie and take five hundred dollars from a church!

"Well," I said, "I'm sorry to tell you, but he did nothing. As you can see, everything is old and dirty. New parts would be clean, the felts would be white. The strings and tuning pins would be shiny, not rusted." I felt sorry for him, being responsible for such a difficult state of affairs.

He was shaking his head in confused bewilderment. "Why would someone do something like that?" he finally said. Then he looked at me. "We can't tell anyone."

"What?" I asked. I was ready to form a lynch mob and go find the guy. At least there should be a discrete conversation with the local prosecutor about pressing charges for fraud. "Why?"

"Well," he said, a pained look on his face, "it would be terrible for the donor who paid for this to find out her money was wasted. She would be devastated. We can't let it be known."

I thought about his situation. There was nothing to do, I supposed. I didn't want to argue with him, although I would have thought the donor would have preferred to know and enjoy a prosecution. I had to defer to his judgment. He knew her; I didn't. I wondered how much of what I had shown and explained about the piano to the first pastor was ever communicated to this one. He seemed quite stunned with the predicament.

"Okay, I won't take any action on this myself, but I would really like to." I was disgusted with the situation. He thanked me, clasping his hands over mine in an emotional handshake. He asked me to please tune it the best I could, and he would work with the church board on buying a new piano. He'd be sure to call me, he said, before anything else was decided. That was six years ago, and no one has called.

Some churches where I work are towering temples, spread in cut stone or brick wings over a city block. The sanctuaries of these palaces to God reach high into the sky, as though any worshipper might look up during services at the vaulted ceiling and almost see God leaning over the edge of the sloping roof line. The pews are padded with comfortable cushions, upholstered with fine fabric which is color-coordinated with the long thick velvet draperies and plush carpets.

The musical instruments in these churches include several high-quality pianos, six-, seven-, or nine-foot grands, and pipe organs that are built into recesses of the tall, wood-paneled walls behind the platform. There are bell choirs, miniature orchestras, adult and children's choruses, not to mention digital mixers and P.A. systems. Praising the Lord is a major production.

Full staff in several offices of these churches means I can come and go anytime without having to make special arrangements to meet someone who can unlock the door. In return for the high volume of their business and convenience of servicing, I give a generous discount to these churches. It is a good business relationship.

But I have a hesitation about my work there, not so much that I question the work but more that I am uneasy being there. The magnificence of the buildings and furnishings worry me, having been brought up in a small church where the strictest possible interpretation of the Bible has made me uncomfortably aware of the prohibitions against building temples and rich kingdoms on earth. It's as if the extravagance of the surroundings might serve as some kind of lightning rod to bring down the flaming wrath of God Almighty. I don't want to be around when that happens. When tuning there, I'll sometimes involuntarily cringe when these thoughts cross my mind, and I hurry to finish.

I've tuned at one-room churches all over the region, buildings that were raised around the turn of the century by hands of people who lived within wagon distance. Typically one of these buildings served as a school during the week, a community building whenever one was needed, and as a church every Sunday. A traveling preacher might unload his wagon to stay at a local house and preach there a spell, or a local man might read from the Good Book and lead the singing.

There was usually a big wood-burning stove set in the middle of the center aisle, so everyone could benefit from the fire on cold winter days. Tall windows that line the side walls let in plenty of light, and latter-day improvements, such as electricity and gas heat, are tacked on only in some. Almost all of these old buildings required the use of outdoor toilets, but fancier ones had a privy for men and one for women instead of just one to serve both.

I have been called to churches in places with fabulous names: Locust Grove, Walnut Grove, Elm Springs, Cave Springs, Dripping Springs, Hogeye, Devil's Den, Sulphur City, Sunset, Mt. Comfort, Little Flock, Antioch, Cane Hill, Nob Hill, Cincinnati, and Fifty-Six. Most of the time I go in with no one there because the door is never locked. The ancient handmade pews sit unevenly on well-worn bare oak floors, the pulpit is not fancy, and the crusty old upright piano weighs close to a ton. Who would steal anything here?

I had one such job at a church that sat about nine miles down a dirt road south of a small town which itself was an hour's drive from Fayetteville. I had scheduled other appointments in that town for the morning, ate a great lunch at the local diner, and relaxed as I headed south toward the church. It was a fine June day, humid and threatening thunderstorms with murky clouds that obscured the sky, casting leaden shadows onto the forested hillsides and overgrown ravines.

The rocky road curved past high outcroppings of gray limestone and black slate, around low bends where wet-weather creeks tumbled over wide ledges of stone and passed underneath the roadway at narrow concrete bridges. The smooth curves of the cleared, newly greened hills were interrupted by jagged mosaics of darker woods, left to grow in places too steep or rough for pasture, or owned by those who valued the land for the woods more than for grazing cattle. Tall, dense clumps of oak, hickory, locust, cherry, and walnut were under-layered with sumac, cedar, dogwood, redbud, serviceberry, and thunderbriar — a mix of all possible shades of green, brown, gray, and red.

I inched down a steep slope where the rock ridges marred the road surface, scaled down by repeated encounters with road graders to form a washboard of rock and dirt, the ditches steeply washed out on either side. The brash red clay exposures in the ditch washes were textured with protruding seams of tan sandstone, then further down by shambling outbreaks of black shale. As I guided my car slowly down the rough corrugations, I glanced up at the vista in front of me, the layered distances of hill after hill fading from the rich colors up close to the deep blue hills in the middle distance then to the faintly blue-gray hills sitting in a third layer back. Two turkey buzzards circled in sharp black outline against the clouded sky, their fluted wing tips tilting and curling as the late spring breeze shifted, their heads dropped and focused toward some rotting flesh on the distant ground.

Old barbed-wire fences ran alongside the road, sagging in spots where a bold calf could climb through to have adventures in the lush grasses of the ditch without having to stray too far from mother and her warm milk. Every mile or so I passed old farmhouses, their white-painted wooden frames grown outward from the first narrow two rooms with added side rooms, a back kitchen with the newfangled plumbing tucked under the gently sloping shingled roof. Often, a rusty brown creosote stain flowed down across the shingles from the top of the brick or stone chimney, running to the low edge of the roof where it abruptly stopped at the unguttered edge.

They all had porches, as most Ozark houses do, furnished with a chair or two, maybe an upright freezer and a half rick of split white oak firewood, a pair of muddy boots, and the requisite ugly dog. Rippling out from the houses in ever wider rings were the flower beds, woodshed, well house, chicken coop, the garden, the barn, tractor shed, larger stacks of firewood, old appliances, tractor implements, a rusting pickup wheelless on concrete blocks, stacks of used sheet metal, a pond, and a panorama of the woods and hills stretching off in paler purplish blues to meet the overcast sky. I was enjoying my drive.

I finally arrived at the church, set back from the road by

enough room to encourage any driver to park randomly along the graveled yard. The land rose slightly toward the church, and on behind the church it rose even higher to meet the woods that covered the rest of the hillside with dark mysteries of green. I drove up close to the front steps, where the high rock foundation stood behind the cement steps and framed porch that was centered in the front of the building. The wood siding was thick with old white paint, the double doors slightly warped from their years in the elements and topped by a weather-beaten sign that announced: Grapevine Nob - 1919.

I stepped inside, smoothing my clothes and hair that the rising warm wind had thrashed between the car and church door, and immediately smelled musty hymn books, Old Spice, and the remnants of wood fires, all mixed with the humid, wet smell of the coming storm. I walked toward the front, passing seats where the regulars left things, some marked with a fancy crocheted pillow or a box of tissues, a few with selected children's toys or a folded blanket.

The walls were unevenly plastered, a few areas marked with tan water stains or peeling white paint. A simple pulpit stood in the center between the massive upright piano on the left wall and a couple of chairs on the right wall, perhaps where someone could sit to play guitar or shake a tambourine during the singing. The strange light of the gathering storm glared in through the slightly warped glass of the tall, framed windows. I made a note to keep my eye on a small nest of red wasps that was lodged in the upper corner of one.

I slid the rickety bench away from the front of the piano and used it as a table to hold the things from the piano's top lid: faded hymn books, a pencil, a pair of praying hands carved life-sized in dark wood, a battered arrangement of plastic orange lilies, and the broken painted-white cover plate from the light switch by the nearby side door. Above the top of the piano on the rough texture of the white wall hung an eight-by-ten pasteboard picture of Jesus, his glowing face looking up toward a bright light in the dark clouds, his hands clasped in prayer as he kneeled at a large rock, probably meant to be his last prayer in the garden of Gethsemane. The coloring of the picture was cracked in places, showing the gray fiber of the paper underneath, and the edges of the picture were thickened and sponged out from humidity and handling.

The piano had stood stalwart there as dusty decades rolled by, its creamy ivories worn from the repeated touch of emotional hands. The cabinet was blackened in its old thick varnish, the obscured pattern of ribbon mahogany grain faintly visible across the upper front and side panels. The brass of the right pedal was worn half off in a gleaming cut, contrasting the tarnished brass on the rest of the pedals where no one's foot bothered to stomp in the rhythms of the gospel songs.

Prepared finally to tune it, and accepting that my work would be a full step below pitch to best suit the long-set state of the instrument's ancient strings, I heard the low rumble of thunder break down the hillside. It was a cozy feeling, to be gathered inside the venerable building, working yet again in my chosen task to craft a compromise between the unattainable, stark ideal of a perfectly tempered scale and the stubborn, singular voice proscribed in this particular set of strings, this cracked spruce soundboard, this mechanism's mathematics, arbitrarily set forth by a simple man engineering the best-known design of his day seventy years before now, while Mother Nature worked her will outside.

As I tuned, wresting first one rusty tuning pin and then another, the thunderstorm boiled up outside, framed for me like Renaissance art through the nearby windows. Sudden gusts of wind crashed through the wildly bending trees wet with the sheets of rain. The water ran off the windows and collected in rushing brown rivulets that raced down the sloping grassy ground toward the wide, worn ditches behind my car along the gravel road. The steady cadence of rain pounded the resonant sheet-metal roof, at times drowning out the notes I struck in the continued process of tuning.

Slowly the storm passed, and I neared the end of my work. Soon it was no more than a diminishing rumble echoing back from the progressing cloud bank, now bestowing its wrath on lands farther east. A sprinkling of rain still ran off the eaves as I pulled a corner of the bench forward so I could sit and play a few phrases to check the results of my labor. I propped open one of the tattered hymn books to page eighty-three, hearing the words to the verse in my mind along with the notes I played: "Amazing grace, how sweet the sound that saves a wretch like me. . . . " The throat of this masterful old beast opened wide, pouring forth rich sound that overcame me, swept me along in tremulous, swelling harmonies. "I once was lost but now I'm found," the music went on, my hands moving by themselves as the vibrant sounds roared in my ears, " . . . was blind but now I see."

The last simple chords were sublime in their resolution, a shimmer of the piano's anthem that seemed to breathe out life into the room, rushing past me in waves. At that same instant, the clouds from the storm broke open and sunlight poured through the wavering wet glass of the tall windows to join the echoes of the final chords. It was as if the music and light were joined in some infinitely powerful manifestation of all that was true and beautiful. I was left breathless, in gooseflesh, for long, perfect seconds before the moment passed.

Hillsong

Denele Campbell

"Hillsong" is routinely used by Ms. Campbell
to check the piano after the tuning.